THE ART AND ARTISTS OF RUSSIA

I. THE ARCHANGEL MICHAEL. A. Rublev. From Svenigorod, Moscow Province, early 15th century. *Tretyakov Gallery, Moscow.*

THE
ART AND ARTISTS
OF RUSSIA

by Richard Hare

METHUEN & CO LTD

11 NEW FETTER LANE · LONDON EC4

First published 1965

Printed in Great Britain by
W. & J. Mackay & Co Ltd
Chatham, Kent
Colour plates made and printed by
Verlag Aurel Bongers
Recklinghausen, Western Germany

To my wife,
the sculptor and artist
DORA GORDINE

Contents

	List of Illustrations	*page* 11
	Foreword	21
1	Icons and the Byzantine Tradition	23
2	Religious and Secular Silver, and Artistic Work in Precious Metals	68
3	The Birth of Russian Portrait Painting	114
4	Porcelain of the Russian Empire	140
5	Painters of the Early Nineteenth Century	171
6	Painters of the Later Nineteenth and Early Twentieth Centuries	207
7	Some Distinctive Russian Decorative Arts	251
	Select Bibliography	282
	Index	287

Illustrations

COLOUR PLATES

   I   THE ARCHANGEL MICHAEL. A. Rublev, early fifteenth century
frontispiece

  II THE CRUCIFIXION. First half of seventeenth century   *facing page* 23

 III THE RESURRECTION AND DESCENT INTO HELL. Eighteenth century   26

 IV VIRGIN AND CHILD. Late seventeenth or early eighteenth century   30
VIRGIN OF THE SIGN. Eighteenth century   30

  V ST FLORUS AND ST LAVRUS. Eighteenth century   32

 VI THE ROSTOV MIRACLE WORKERS. Second half of eighteenth century   36

 VII ST NICHOLAS THE MIRACLE WORKER. Early nineteenth century   38
ST CATHERINE THE MARTYR. Late eighteenth century   38

VIII Imperial orb. Early seventeenth century   68

 IX Crown of the Empress Anna Ioanovna. c. 1730   70

  X Nielloed silver-gilt pendant. Eighteenth century   74
Enamelled silver box. Seventeenth century   74
Enamelled silver-gilt salt-cellar. Ovchinikov, late nineteenth century   74
Silver-gilt enamelled *kovsch*. Late nineteenth century   74

 XI Enamelled silver cigarette box. Late nineteenth century   76
Enamelled silver-gilt cigarette box. Late nineteenth century   76

 XII Enamelled silver-gilt tea-caddy. Fabergé, late nineteenth century
facing plate 55

XIII Enamelled silver-gilt beaker. Ovchinikov, late nineteenth century   57

XIV Silver-gilt tea-caddy. Lyubavin, late nineteenth century   61

XV   Dish with exotic birds and flowers. Imperial Porcelain Factory, c. 1840   *facing page* 140
Dish from dinner-service presented by Alexander I to his sister. Imperial Factory, c. 1810   140

XVI   Part of a tea-service. Kornilov, mid-nineteenth century   *facing page* 144
Part of a tea and coffee-service. Safronov, c. 1830   144

XVII   Chocolate cup. Kozlov, c. 1840   146
Large cup. Imperial Factory, c. 1820   146

XVIII   Plates from dinner-services ordered by Nicholas I. Imperial Factory, c. 1830   148

XIX   Girl in blue trousers. Gardner, mid-nineteenth century   150
Lady in red *sarafan*. Kornilov, mid-nineteenth century   150
Young gentleman with a dog and a young lady in a pink dress. Popov, mid-nineteenth century   150

XX   Sweetmeat dish. Popov, c. 1840   150
Bread and salt plate. Popov, c. 1850.   150

XXI   Monumental vase. Imperial Factory, c. 1860   154

XXII   Plate from Raphael service. Imperial Factory, c. 1885   *facing plate* 90
Plate with fruit and flowers. Imperial Factory, c. 1840   90

XXIII   Porcelain Easter eggs. Late nineteenth century   96

XXIV   PRINCESS BARATINSKY. A. Bryulov, early nineteenth century   *facing page* 176

XXV   A MOSCOW TEA-HOUSE. V. Kustodiev, late nineteenth century   224

XXVI   Four painted boxes. Lukutin, mid and late nineteenth century   251

XXVII   Three chairs in Karelian birch. c. 1810   254
Sofa in Karelian birch. c. 1810   254

XXVIII   Three painted papier mâché boxes. Lukutin, nineteenth century   256

XXIX   Two papier mâché boxes. Lukutin, late nineteenth century   258

XXX   Two painted boxes. Church of St Basil, Moscow   260
View of the Kremlin from Moscow River. Lukutin, mid-nineteenth century   260

XXXI   Painted boxes. Lukutin and Vishnyakov, mid-nineteenth century   262

XXXII   Two large papier mâché boxes. Lukutin, early nineteenth century   262

MONOCHROME PLATES

pages 41 to 67

1   THE VIRGIN OF VLADIMIR. Brought from Constantinople to Kiev in the early twelfth century

2   HEAD OF AN ANGEL. Twelfth century

3   THE APOSTLES ST PETER AND ST PAUL. Twelfth century

4   THE VIRGIN OF THE SIGN. Thirteenth century

5   ST JOHN THE EVANGELIST WITH ST GEORGE AND ST BLAISE. Thirteenth century

6   THE VIRGIN MARY. Theophanes the Greek, 1405

7   NOAH. Theophanes the Greek, 1378

8   Frescoes, Therapont Monastery. Dionysius, between 1500 and 1502

9   THE ASCENSION. Second quarter of fifteenth century

10   ST FLORUS AND ST LAVRUS. Late fifteenth century

11   THE OLD TESTAMENT TRINITY. c. 1600

12   THE RESURRECTION. Sixteenth century

13   OUR LADY OF THE BURNING BUSH. Late fifteenth century

14   ST JOHN THE BAPTIST. Early seventeenth century

15   ST JOHN THE WARRIOR. Early seventeenth century

16   PORTABLE ICONOSTASIS. Mid-sixteenth century

17   THE ARCHANGEL GABRIEL SURROUNDED BY ANGELS. Late sixteenth century

18   VIRGIN AND CHILD. Seventeenth century

19   VIRGIN OF VLADIMIR. Sixteenth century version

20   THE CRUCIFIXION. Seventeenth century

21   ICON OF THE VERNICLE. Simon Ushakov, 1673

22   VIRGIN AND CHILD. Simon Ushakov, later half of seventeenth century

23   CHRIST ENTHRONED. Nikita Pavlov, mid-seventeenth century

24   ST JOHN WITH THE WINGS. Early seventeenth century

25   THE DEAD CHRIST WITH THE VIRGIN MARY AND ST JOHN. Eighteenth century

26 CROWNED VIRGIN AND CHILD. Eighteenth century
Icon with scenes from the life of the Virgin. Seventeenth century

27A DORMITION OF THE VIRGIN. Mid-nineteenth century

27B ST PANTELEIMON. Last decade of nineteenth century

pages 79 to 113

28 Silver-gilt gospel cover. c. 1534

29 Silver-gilt Zion. Fourteenth century

30 Crystal barrel in silver-gilt setting. Probably fifteenth century

31 Oval casket for holding consecrated bread or relics. Mid-seventeenth century

32 Gold plate of the Tsar Alexei Mikhailovich. Mid-seventeenth century

33 Gold nielloed dish. 1561

34 Lid of silver sarcophagus of Prince Dmitri. 1630

35A Silver *bratina* of the Emperor Ivan IV (the Terrible). Sixteenth century

35B *Bratina.* Mid-nineteenth century

36 Gold and jewelled *kovsch.* 1618

37 Oval *kovsch* in massive silver. 1709

38 Engraved *kovsch.* Fabergé, late nineteenth century

39 Silver-gilt cup and cover. 1733

40 Silver-gilt cup and cover. c. 175?

41 Silver dish. Mid-seventeenth century

42 Enamelled silver-gilt gospel cover. 1729

43 Silver-gilt altar-gates (*Royal Doors of the Priesthood*). 1784

44 Miniature of Princess Evgenia Yusupov. Late eighteenth century
Gold snuff-box. Early nineteenth century
Gold box. 1853

45 Nielloed silver tea-caddy. 1775

46 Massive silver tankard. 1800
Nielloed silver-tray. Late eighteenth century

47 Russian Church chalices. Seventeenth and eighteenth centuries

48 Silver-gilt jewelled chalice. Eighteenth century

49 Cigarette box. Early nineteenth century
Snuff-box. Late eighteenth century

ILLUSTRATIONS

Nielloed box with landscape scene. Mid-nineteenth century

50 Nielloed box, the Palace Square, Petersburg. Early nineteenth century
Nielloed box, architectural scene. c. 1825
Nielloed box, Moscow Kremlin. c. 1850
Box with architectural scene. Late eighteenth century
Nielloed box, Falconet's statue of Peter the Great, Petersburg. Early nineteenth century

51A Silver-gilt coffee-pot. 1864
Covered jug. Sazykov, 1856

51B Casket. Early nineteenth century

52A Casket and glass-holder in silver filigree. Early nineteenth century

52B Three beakers illustrating changes of style in half a century, 1745. 1771. 1802

53 Five glass-holders. Nineteenth century

54 Silver-gilt teapot. Mid-nineteenth century
Two chalice-shaped cloisonné enamel wine-cups. c. 1870
Painted silver cigarette box. c. 1870

55 Covered pot engraved with human figures. Mid-nineteenth century

56 Silver-gilt cup and cover. Mid-nineteenth century

57 Wine jug with cover. 1856

58 Massive engraved coffee-pot. Sazykov, 1861

59 Teapot and hexagonal tray. Mid-nineteenth century

60 Cup and cover with high-relief *troika*. Late nineteenth century

61A Silver filigree fan. c. 1850

61B Teapot and milk-jug. Fabergé, late nineteenth century

62 Pair of silver serving spoons. Fabergé, late nineteenth century

pages 122 to 139

63 TSAR FYODOR ALEXEIVICH. Late seventeenth century

64 PRINCE SCOPIN SHUISKY. First half of seventeenth century

65 Portraits of Peter the Great and Catherine I. Early eighteenth century

66 ANNA PETROVNA, elder daughter of Peter the Great. Before 1727

67 THE TSAREVICH ALEXEI, SON OF PETER THE GREAT. Tannauer, early eighteenth century

68 COUNTESS APRAKSIN. A. Antropov, mid-eighteenth century

69 THE EMPEROR PETER III. A. Antropov

70 PRINCE GRIGORY ORLOV. S. Rokotov, mid-eighteenth century

71A COUNTESS E. R. VORONTSOV. L. Tocqué, mid-eighteenth century

71B AFANASIA NESTEROV. M. Chibanov (serf artist), late eighteenth century

72A PRINCE GRIGORY POTEMKIN. J. B. Lampi (*père*), second half of eighteenth century

72B CATHERINE THE GREAT. A. Roslin, late eighteenth century

73 COUNTESS KUSHELEV AND CHILDREN. V. Borovikovsky, eighteenth century

74 THE PRINCESSES HELEN AND ALEXANDRA GAGARIN. V. Borovikovsky

75 THE METROPOLITAN MICHAEL DESNITSKY (1761–1818). V. Borovikovsky

76 PRINCESS DASHKOV. D. Levitsky, second half of eighteenth century

77 ALEXANDRA LEVSHIN. D. Levitsky

78 CATHERINE NELIDOV. D. Levitsky

79 IVAN RIBEAUPIERRE. D. Levitsky

80 AGATHOCLÉE POLTORATSKY. D. Levitsky

81 Cup with cover and saucer. Imperial Factory, first half of eighteenth century   *facing page* 142

pages 156 to 170

82A Kirghiz man and woman. Gardner, nineteenth century

82B Figures of a Mordovinian and a Cheremetian woman. Gardner Factory, late eighteenth or early nineteenth century

83A Plate painted with armorial symbols. Imperial Factory, c. 1830

83B Champagne cooler. Imperial Factory, eighteenth century

84 Porcelain candelabra. Second half of eighteenth century

85 Coffee-pot. Popov Factory, early nineteenth century

86 Three porcelain figures. Gardner, early nineteenth century

87 Boy carrying a potted plant. Gardner, late eighteenth century. Russian dandy. Kornilov Factory, c. 1840

88 Vase with Empire style handles. Imperial Factory, c. 1820

89 Monumental vase. Imperial Factory, c. 1830

90A Plate with portrait of Anna Petrovna. Imperial Factory, second half of eighteenth century
Plate with flowers, butterflies and bird. Imperial Factory, c. 1840

90B Plate with woman carrying bundle. Gardner, c. 1800
Plate with Yakut woman. Imperial Factory, c. 1810

91A Teapot. Imperial Factory, mid-nineteenth century
Coffee-pot with cipher of Alexander III. Imperial Factory, late nineteenth century

91B Hot-water jug. Kornilov, mid-nineteenth century
Coffee-pot. Imperial Factory, c. 1840

92 Sauce-boat and dish. Imperial Factory, c. 1840

93 Ceremonial bread and salt plate. Mid-nineteenth century
Plate with gold foliage border. Imperial Factory, c. 1825

94 Teapot depicting Alexander Column in Palace Square, Petersburg. Batenin, early nineteenth century

95 Vase with architectural scene of Petersburg. Imperial Factory, c. 1820

96 Large porcelain jardinière. Imperial Factory, c. 1870

pages 188 to 206

97 V. SUKHANOV. A. Egorov, 1812

98 THE SPINNER. V. Tropinin, c. 1820

99 SELF-PORTRAIT. O. Kiprensky, c. 1808

100 Y. DAVIDOV. O. Kiprensky, early nineteenth century

101 THE DANCER, K. TELESHEVA. O. Kiprensky, 1828

102 POOR LISA. O. Kiprensky, 1827

103 HARVESTING, SUMMER. A. Venetsianov, 1830

104 SLEEPING SHEPHERD. A. Venetsianov, 1824

105A DRAWING OF A PEASANT. P. Barbe, 1824

105B HEAD OF A PEASANT. A. Venetsianov, 1825

106 PORTRAIT OF THE ARTIST'S SON. V. Tropinin, c. 1820

107 PORTRAIT OF E. MILYUKOV. G. Soroka (peasant artist), c. 1846

108 YOUNG GIRL PLACING A CANDLE IN THE CHURCH. G. Mikhailov, c. 1842

109   SELF-PORTRAIT. K. Bryulov, c. 1820

110   z. HITROVO. K. Bryulov, 1832

111   THE LAST DAY OF POMPEII (detail). K. Bryulov, 1833

112   ITALIAN NOON. K. Bryulov, 1827

113   THE SHISHMAREV SISTERS. K. Bryulov, 1839

114   THE COSSACK FEDYUSHKIN. Prince G. Gagarin, 1840

115A THE APPEARANCE OF THE MESSIAH BEFORE THE PEOPLE (detail). A. Ivanov, early nineteenth century

115B NUDE BOY. A. Ivanov, c. 1852

116A The Artist; 'No, I won't exhibit; they will never understand!' From a drawing by P. Fedotov, mid-nineteenth century   *facing page* 208

116B 'Oh, what a hard life we merchants have!' Unknown artist, mid-nineteenth century   208

pages 230 to 250

117   THE MAJOR'S COURTSHIP. P. Fedotov, 1848

118A THE NINTH WAVE. I. Ayvasovsky, mid-nineteenth century

118B VIEW OF THE WINTER PALACE. Lithograph from the painting by Vorobyov, early nineteenth century   *text page* 212

119   FOUNTAINS IN THE GARDEN OF PETERHOF. From an early nineteenth century water-colour

120   VIEW OF THE PASHKOV HOUSE. From an early nineteenth century engraving

121   THE BOYARINYA MOROZOVA. V. Surikov, c. 1882

122   ON THE BOULEVARD. V. G. Makovsky, mid-nineteenth century

123   THE RAVENS HAVE ARRIVED. A. Savrasov, 1871

124A PEASANT GIRL. A. Stryelkovsky, 1856

124B GYPSY GIRL. A. Harlamov, mid-nineteenth century

125   THE VILLAGE FUNERAL. V. Perov, 1865

126   THE TEA DRINKING. V. Perov, 1862

127   A MOHAMMEDAN SERVANT. V. Vereshchagin, late nineteenth century

128   THE COMPOSER, M. MUSSORGSKY. I. Repin, 1881

129   PEASANT BOY IN A VILLAGE SCHOOL. N. Bogdanov-Byelsky, late nineteenth century

ILLUSTRATIONS

130   VERA MAMONTOV. V. Serov, 1887

131A   THE YOUNG F. CHALIAPIN. V. Serov, 1905

131B   M. MOROZOV. V. Serov, 1887

132   SKETCH OF ANNA PAVLOVA. V. Serov, 1909

133   GIRL AGAINST THE BACKGROUND OF A PERSIAN CARPET.
       M. Vrubel, late nineteenth century

134   THE DEMON. M. Vrubel, 1890

135   THE POET, V. BRYUSOV. M. Vrubel

136   Sketch of a costume for Cherapin's ballet. *Narcissus.* L. Bakst, early
       twentieth century

137   Design for a scene in Turgenev's play *A Month in the Country.*
       M. Dobujinsky, early twentieth century

138   Wooden *kovsch.* Early nineteenth century   *text page* 252

pages 264 to 281

139A   Boxwood carving of the Last Supper. Mid-nineteenth century

139B   Carved wooden mould for stamping gingerbread. Late eighteenth
        century

140   Carved wooden picture frame. A serf artist, first half of nineteenth
        century

141   Chairs and table painted with traditional designs. Mid-nineteenth century

142A   Tula steel fireplace. Late eighteenth century

142B   Tula steel chair. Eighteenth century

143   Table in gilded carved wood. Late eighteenth century

144   Double-fronted chest in ebony. 1873

145   Pottery *kvass*-jug. Eighteenth century

146   Pottery *kvass*-jug. Mid-nineteenth century

147   Pair of bronze-gilt figures. Second half of nineteenth century

148A   Two dancing peasant boys in bronze-gilt. Second half of nineteenth
        century

148B   Two traditional carved and painted wooden arches, placed over
        horses' necks

        Bronze *troika.* E. A. Lanseré, late nineteenth century

149   The Emperor Alexander II. Bronze by an unknown artist

150 Ivory portrait-bust of the Empress Maria Fyodorovna. 1882

151 Carved ivory goblet. Eighteenth century

152A Two cut-glass goblets. Eighteenth century

152B Two cut-glass oblong decanters

153 Specimens of glass from the Imperial Glass Factory, Petersburg. From late eighteenth to mid-nineteenth century

154 Engraved wine jug. Mid-nineteenth century
     Liqueur decanter. Early nineteenth century

155A Massive malachite vase

155B Tray in dark green nephrite. Fabergé, late nineteenth century

156 Pair of malachite candelabra and *tazzas*, seen against imperial tapestry carpet. Nineteenth century

Foreword

People who have long since paid tribute to Tchaikovsky's music, the Diaghilev Ballet and the Moscow Art Theatre, remain puzzled about the Russian visual arts. Throughout the Kiev, Moscow and Petersburg periods of Russian history, foreign artists and craftsmen of many nationalities came to work in Russia, where they imparted their skill to eager native pupils. Even some so-called national peasant arts strikingly resemble those of Scandinavia, and many works in precious metal derived their motifs from Persia and northern India. From all that strange complexity, where foreign immigrants responded to the stimulus of a new environment, some Russian traits of character emerged. But their distinct artistic individuality can be felt and recognized rather than rigidly defined. As John Ruskin observed: great nations write their own biographies in three separate volumes, – a book of words, a book of deeds, and a book of art – but of these three only the last deserves to be fully trusted. It speaks for itself.

Russian art rose to its highest point in periods of strenuous emulation. Then it was not self-centred; it pursued no sensational novelty and pointed no topical moral. Therefore it flourished, both when it set itself religious standards, derived from the Byzantine Empire, and later when it transferred its reverence to that exhilarating many-sided endeavour, more recently set in motion by the civilized countries of Western Europe.

Indeed this alert and eagerly receptive flair, allied with constant and generous admiration of gifted outsiders, made the best Russian art refreshingly free from self-consciously national traits of character. Dostoyevsky praised it in the work of Pushkin as a Russian imaginative response to the talent of *past ages and foreign genius*. This faculty proved it had the power to reincarnate within itself the finest qualities of alien countries, without abandoning its native individuality. Tolstoy, who felt deeply alarmed by later nineteenth century developments in taste, sought salvation in a vigorous traditional folk-art, which alone in Russia had remained immune from the demoralizing sophistication of the modern West. For he believed that the so-called 'modern' art of Western Europe had grown anaemic, debauched or slovenly, and was infecting other countries, including Russia, with its own disease. They both believed that art was doomed, if artists failed to revere and emulate the skilled technique, ideals, and honest striving of their predecessors.

Be that as it may, there can be no doubt that these enlightened Russians took art seriously, felt that their country had created, or tried to create, something substantial in the past, and could still contribute to the spiritual development of human beings. Of course their claims did not fully correspond to facts. But the true nature of what Russia gave to the world of visual art has not yet received in other countries the attention which it merits. This introductory survey can only start to fill that gap, by giving (with many inevitable omissions) a brief account of various arts which flourished in the Russian Empire, some information about its leading artists, and the environment which shaped them, and by selecting examples of their most characteristic work. I have been obliged to omit architecture and monumental sculpture. Bearing in mind the need to illustrate distinctive Russian arts and their links with Byzantium or Western Europe, I have had photographed for the first time many beautiful and significant objects, not previously publicized, which may be unfamiliar to Western art connoisseurs, because they are scantily represented in Western art collections.

I owe a debt of gratitude to the editor of *The Connoisseur* for permission to republish some material from articles, which I originally wrote for that journal, to Mrs Merriweather Post May for the unrestricted use of specially taken photographs from her unique collection of Russian art in Washington, D.C., to Marvin Ross for his generosity in providing me with factual information, to Nikolay Andreyev (formerly of the Kondakov Institute, Prague) for expert advice about the section devoted to Russian icons, and to the State Historical Museum in Moscow, and the State Museum of Ceramics at Kuskovo, for help with illustrations. I also wish to thank Miss Dorothy Galton for reading the proofs.

For a number of superb photographs I am indebted to the highly skilled staff of the Victoria and Albert Museum, London, in particular to Peter Macdonald and J. C. Strand, whose efficient and courteous collaboration has greatly helped my work.

II. THE CRUCIFIXION. Moscow School, first half of 17th century.

CHAPTER ONE

Icons and the Byzantine Tradition

Russian religious art fared none the worse for being international in character from the start. Whether in mosaic, fresco painting, sacred vessels of jewelled and enamelled precious metals, or in the painted wooden panels called icons, it developed as a living branch of the Greek Byzantine art, from which it sprang, and by which it was nourished during the first four centuries of its existence.

According to Nestor's chronicle, the enterprising Vladimir, Prince of Kiev, sent emissaries to various countries, and instructed them to report to him faithfully on the rival merits of available organized religions. In fact, Vladimir was trying hard to find a practical religion, which could best help an enlightened, hard-working ruler to capture the imagination of unruly subjects, and keep them under firm control. The envoy who visited Constantinople was spell-bound by the splendour of the festive service which he attended in the Cathedral of Saint Sophia. His report about this awe-inspiring religion was so much more impressive than the others, that Vladimir promptly selected Orthodox Christianity as the most suitable faith to hold together disorderly Russia, and commanded his unstable but obedient subjects to be baptized. In this way Vladimir, in the year A.D. 988, imposed both official Christianity and its ancillary art upon his malleable country.

Together with an influx of priests from the Byzantine Empire, came architects, icons and icon painters, whose Russian disciples were taught to copy with meticulous reverence a number of Byzantine prototypes. But this proved to be easier said than done. For the prototypes were far from static, and often inaccessible to Russians. In the eighth century triumphant inconoclast fanatics had destroyed the majority of existing icons throughout the Byzantine Empire. When religious imagery returned to favour, the tradition of Byzantine style was turning towards a distinct but peculiar blend, which the greatest Russian art historian, N. Kondakov, termed the Greco-Oriental, since it introduced many motifs drawn from the Orthodox Church in Egypt and Asia Minor. It so happened that this period of artistic revival coincided with the religious adornment of the first important Russian churches in Kiev and Novgorod in the eleventh century.

Though icon painting always remained formal, hieratic and architecturally composed, it could not possibly become merely geometrical or abstract, because, in attempting to represent what belonged to a separate spiritual world, it never dreamed of renouncing the basic physical and natural forms of life. Far from being repudiated, the latter were deliberately stylized or adapted, to fulfil strict ecclesiastical requirements, and make the physical element serve as a proper vehicle for conveying pure religious feelings.

For the aesthetic faith of Eastern Christianity demanded unconditionally that a spiritual body should always be in conflict with a carnal one. Moreover, it encouraged the beholder of religious images to attain, during his earthly life, through a constant visual reminder of sacred personages, events, and thoughts, that actual communion with an unseen supernatural world, about which other Churches taught rather the post-human fulfilment after death.

Whereas in Western countries the visual image was chiefly tolerated by the churches, through serving as 'the bible of the ignorant', in the East the image itself remained vital, all-important, and irreplaceable by any verbal language. It bore witness, in its own inimitable manner, no less than scripture itself, to the newly established sanctity of the human body, imparted to it solely by Christ's incarnation in human form. It is noteworthy that in Russia portrait icons of Christ, his Mother, the major saints and martyrs, exerted the strongest personal appeal and were always the most popular and beloved. The icons representing Church festivals, or symbolic illustrations of orthodox Christian doctrine, aroused less fervour among their beholders. At the same time, in order to maintain its authority unshaken, the religious image had to reflect an *immutability* of natural law in human kinship with the divine. Therefore the Orthodox believer opposed the roving and pagan sensuality encouraged by the Renaissance in Europe. And the self-centred modern craving for artistic 'originality' and petty individual self-assertion were equally alien to his aspirations.

But such stern demands imposed an unduly heavy burden on the icon painter. To become worthy of fulfilling his function as a visual intermediary between God and man, he was expected to live like a dedicated being, a humble and ascetic servant of God. The words of Plotinus were applied to him: 'Only when a man is perfect shall the vision of God be vouchsafed to him. He has the only eye that sees

24

the mighty beauty. If the eye that ventures on the vision be dimmed by vice, impure or weak, then it can see nothing.'[1] We have no convincing evidence that many icon painters lived like exemplary Christian saints or hermits, though a fair number, like Rublev, were monks. But we know that most patriotic Russian purists shared the dark superstitions of the seventeenth century Old Believers, in imagining that the vital religious essence of icon painting was bound to evaporate with the first profane touch of any more skilfully realistic rendering of the physical human form.

In Russia the devout veneration for icons went incomparably further than it had done in Byzantium, not only in Church ritual, but in the demand for devotional pictures to be hung, worshipped and prayed to in private places. Although it was far from being a spontaneous growth, but a foreign symbol, chosen and forced upon Russians by their princely rulers, the icon somehow grew into the chief visible manifestation of Russian religious thought and feeling, which has survived ever since the Middle Ages. This factor alone, apart from their own remote beauty, should impart to icons a unique historical interest. Yet for a long time they were regarded coldly as mere cult objects, stereotyped accessories, peculiar to the ritual of the Orthodox Church.

One can hardly blame European and American connoisseurs for their relative neglect of this branch of Russian art, when one recalls that only since the beginning of the present century did educated Russians themselves begin to discover the great artistic quality of their better icons. And they waited until 1913 (to celebrate the tercentenary of the Romanov dynasty) before they organized the first comprehensive large-scale exhibition of these paintings in Moscow.

In the later nineteenth century Old Believers of the merchant class, who, after the Great Schism, had zealously maintained their customs, became keen collectors of ancient icons, though they still valued them as historical and religious documents rather than as independent works of art with intrinsic quality and style. But these discriminating collectors created a new demand for scientific cleaning and more careful investigation of icons, however crude or monotonous they might be. That preliminary sifting led to a gradual recognition of the bewildering variety, startling artistic inequality, but occasionally very high aesthetic value, of Russian religious painting. The latter remains the point of view from which many people, outside the Orthodox Church, are likely to approach the subject.

[1] See *The Birth of Western Painting*, by R. Byron and D. Talbot Rice, New York, 1931, p. 95.

Russian icons were normally painted on panels of seasoned wood, with two diagonal strips of wood inserted in the back, to prevent warping. The panels were first covered with a white priming, sometimes laid over with fine cloth, or a gold-leaf background, and were then painted with tempera colours, mixed with yolk of egg and diluted with *kvass* (a fermented drink made from fruit or rye-bread). Finally they were varnished with boiled linseed oil. Inevitably they got soiled and darkened from the soot produced by lighted candles and clouds of incense. The paint flaked off them from the damp atmosphere in churches which were never properly heated, and the wood often rotted. From time to time ignorant local priests, or private owners, had the badly damaged ones perfunctorily repainted and patched up. The expert restorers of the early twentieth century discovered that a lot of the older ones had been repainted several times, and that many original pure colours had turned black or brown under the old linseed-oil varnish.

Unfortunately the basic rule of honest artistic restorers, only to clean and uncover original work, never to add or retouch, was often violated. And because public interest and commercial greed had been aroused, the same thing happened on a smaller scale as did throughout the wider market for Old Master paintings in Europe and America during the nineteenth century. People, who first intended to release an original painting from darkened varnish and later additions, went on to retouch and fill in all the obscured or missing parts. Then a flourishing industry of faked or semi-faked icons grew up, and some collectors were deceived. But those who conscientiously cleaned ancient icons made a rare discovery. They revealed an unexpected radiance of original colour combinations, a glowing purity of tone, and often a subtle expressive draughtsmanship, which first proved to civilized contemporaries the unique qualities of this branch of Russian art. In the case of the famous *Virgin of Vladimir* (the eleventh-century icon brought from Constantinople), which was found to have been restored in the thirteenth, fifteenth and each successive century, the stripping of paint and varnish was done so skilfully that parts of the strata of each century were deliberately preserved.

Although both the fuller human appreciation and systematic study of icons only started in the late nineteenth century under the impetus of a few enthusiastic Russian connoisseurs, even they were tentative in their judgements and attributions, and recognized in their subject a far-reaching and unexplored complexity. Alexander Nazarov, an enlightened industrialist and factory-owner, promoted and personally subsidized the two huge volumes produced by N. Likhachev,

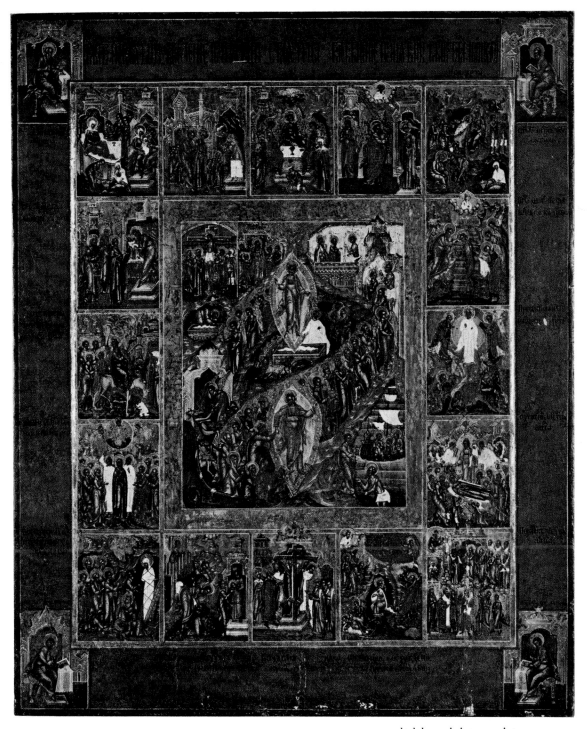

III. THE RESURRECTION AND DESCENT INTO HELL, surrounded by miniature pictures
of Church Festivals. 18th century.

devoted to an illustrated history of Russian icons. But Nazarov explained his motives in a frankly sceptical introduction. 'By means of long and attentive study,' he wrote, 'I have gained an understanding of the peculiar beauty of Chinese and Japanese art, but to my extreme regret I cannot yet grasp either the beauty or the true meaning of Russian icon painting. Yet if the Great Russian people for so many centuries satisfied itself almost exclusively with icons, this form of art can hardly be insignificant.' Another nineteenth-century connoisseur, Professor T. Buslaev, far from admiring uncritically the early primitive icons (the fashion among anti-quarian connoisseurs), complained of the monotony and arrested development shown by customary servility to the semi-Byzantine style, which, he said, fully matched the blank stagnation of ancient Russia in literature and mental activity until her awakening in the seventeenth century.

No Kiev icons painted prior to the Mongol conquest have survived, though some restored frescoes and mosaics have. The best-known early masterpiece still intact is a Byzantine Virgin and Child – the so-called *Virgin of Vladimir* (Plate 1). According to the chronicles, this was brought from Constantinople to Kiev in the twelfth century. Later it was taken to Vladimir, and transferred to Moscow in 1395. It shows from what outstanding Greek originals the early Russian icon painters were fortunate enough to learn. As a *miracle-working* icon it used to be carried in procession at times of national crisis. Copied countless times by several generations of Russian painters, it became partly responsible for that favourite Russian version of the relation between the Holy Mother and Child, the mood of compassionate tenderness, called *Umilenie*, together with the mother's conscious premonition of her son's future martyrdom. The *Head of an Angel*, illustrated here (Plate 2), is a fragment from a damaged fresco in the Dmitrievsky Cathedral at Vladimir. It dates from the later twelfth century, but is less severe than much contemporary Byzantine work. The nose and mouth are softly drawn, and the expression of the face is quietly gentle, without the tragic intensity of sterner Byzantine saints. These well-preserved fresco fragments from a composition of *The Last Judgement* are attributed to immigrant Greek painters and their Russian pupils.

Another early icon, *St Peter and St Paul* (Plate 3), from the Saint Sophia Cathedral at Novgorod, now in the Novgorod museum, maintains the grandiose features of eleventh-century Byzantium, unashamed of its pagan Greek inheritance. The half-starved ascetic Christian had not yet superseded the antique ideal of a physically imposing robed figure, radiating majesty. These figures stand in free equilibrium, their rhythmic geometry enhanced by the parallel stylized folds of flowing robes, executed in the finest *repoussé* silver, similar to some Byzantine ivory carvings. Both painting and silver work date from the late eleventh or early twelfth century, and N. Kondakov accepted them as Byzantine.

The thirteenth-century *Virgin of the Sign* from Yaroslavl, now in the Tretyakov Gallery (Plate 4), has the strictly conceived geometrical grandeur of a similar figure in the frescoes of the Saint Sophia Cathedral at Kiev. But it is less detached and stern, and the frail hands of the Virgin, raised in her prayer for intercession, provide a touching contrast to the monumental composition of her robes. The infant Christ, with a thoughtful domed forehead, represented in a round medallion on her breast, repeats his mother's gesture of supplication for suffering humanity.

After the sack of Kiev by the Tartars, the provincial artistic centres of Pskov, Vladimir-Suzdal, Novgorod, and Yaroslavl, were left for a time to their own devices, cut off from earlier links with Constantinople. Partly through her favourable geographical position and her trade with the Hanseatic towns, and partly through the daring and political skill of her local rulers, Novgorod managed to escape falling to the Tartars, and took over from desecrated Kiev the arduous mission of maintaining against barbaric Asiatic hordes a vital centre for Russian religious art.

The movement away from Byzantine Greek towards a more native Russian idiom (cut off from foreign sources) was hardly an unmixed blessing, and at first involved plain artistic deterioration, as shown by the adoption of crude colouring, more primitively rustic and rough technique (Plate 5). The painters had more frequent recourse to straight lines, flat surfaces and stumpy or elongated figures. That is a marked feature of some Novgorod icons in the fourteenth century. In these churches the Russian type of iconostasis (a whole wall of fixed icons separating the sanctuary from the main body of the church) appears to have been introduced towards the end of the fourteenth century, at first only in two tiers of icons. The three- and four-tiered screen of icons may have started in the fifteenth century, by which time the neo-Hellenic Byzantine renaissance in Constantinople was making itself beneficially felt in the sphere of Russian religious painting. The 'fixed' icons always remained in place and were up to seven feet high, whereas devotional and house icons were moveable and rarely more than two feet high.

Some historic parallels between the courses taken by Russian and Western art can here be discerned more clearly. In the early sixteenth century, icons, both in Novgorod and Moscow, became more animated in expression, more full-bodied in draughtsmanship and in rendering varieties of human emotion – in effect, through the refreshing impact of Byzantine neo-Hellenism, closer to the Italian Renaissance. This revival of pagan classicism *within* Byzantine penetrated to Russian painters through constant pilgrimages, many personal links with the Mount Athos monasteries of Greece, and through the intermediary of South Slav countries, especially Serbia.

But the rival artistic tendencies of the time began to be mastered by a few outstanding artists, whose talent was not blunted by accepting slavery to any single artistic fashion of the day. In the latter half of the fourteenth century Theophanes the Greek, who came to Novgorod from Constantinople, bringing the latest innovations of the Paleologue revival, appears to have rescued the Novgorod school from sinking into the monotony of dull provincial routine. But he also imparted to traditional iconographic themes a strongly individual style, used white lead highlights and cross-hatchings to obtain bold expressive effects, and to dramatize the exalted spiritual feats of Christian saints and biblical heroes (Plates 6 and 7). He astonished his Russian contemporaries by painting freely, without recourse to accepted prototypes.

The masterly Greek, Theophanes, has been unduly overshadowed by his more famous Russian pupil, A. Rublev (who died about 1430). Rublev, a monk in the Spasso-Andryonikov monastery, Moscow, became the dominating artistic figure of that period when Russian religious painting moved towards an arabesque of gentle colour harmonies, reflecting the rhythms of a mystic contemplative style, increasingly remote from hard realities and nature.

From 1395 onwards Theophanes collaborated with Rublev in Moscow in making the iconostasis for the Cathedral of the Annunciation. The remains of frescoes on the west wall of the Cathedral of the Dormition at Vladimir are also attributed to Rublev, together with the well-known *Old Testament Trinity* from the Trinity Sergius Monastery (now in the Tretyakov Gallery). A striking head of the Archangel Michael (Plate I, frontispiece), from Svenigorod, Moscow Province, closely resembles one of the angels in the *Holy Trinity*. It brilliantly illustrates a basic difference between Rublev and two earlier Italian primitives, Cimabue and Duccio, with whom he has been summarily compared. Cimabue paid more heed to rendering naturalistic bone construction, and Duccio went in for softer graded contours. But the severe stylized features and immutable repose of Rublev's Archangel are distinct from both. Rublev thereby showed renewed fidelity to the Byzantine ideal type of the eleventh and twelfth centuries, with its characteristic long sharp nose and small tight-lipped mouth. Only the tall modern *bee-hive* of ornamental curly hair is, in fact, neo-hellenic. The formal expressive beauty of this head is not obtained by any deliberately exciting or dramatic realism, but through the inward and disciplined serenity of a human face which tries to provide a devotional vision of the invisible and eternal.

Undoubtedly Rublev clarified some of the Greek forms, which he inherited, and imbued them with diaphanous purity and graceful inner rhythm, enhanced by an exquisite sense of colour. But even his mellifluous painting comes to the verge of dry abstraction and rigidity. The monasteries of the late fourteenth and early fifteenth century, where Rublev lived and worked, enjoyed a spiritual prestige, prosperity and relative calm, which the violently struggling Muscovite State had not acquired. Rublev's remotely serene and delicate art owes a lot to the supporting environment of an independent, affluent and pious Church, not yet shaken by bitter quarrels between Tsar and Metropolitan, by the Great Schism of the seventeenth century, or by the State's conquest of Church power, followed by the humiliating abasement of the clergy under Peter.

Rublev's chief follower, Dionysius (1440–1502), though he knew how to compose ornate architectural grouping, and founded a school, had already succumbed to feeble mannerisms inherent in the style which he had inherited. The frescoes of the Therapont Monastery, attributed to him and members of his school, illustrate this decline. His human figures, though aiming at intense spirituality, became attenuated, limp and sprawling, while an expression of anaemic detachment stamped their faces with a blank monotony (Plate 8). *The Ascension*, painted by an unknown artist in the same period, is much more tensely and sensitively drawn, and shows a mastery of composition, with its numerous draped figures grouped in complicated rhythmic movement (Plate 9).

The striving for ethereal elegance and refinement, at the expense of simple grandeur or ascetic self-denial, brought the later Novgorod school surprisingly close to the formal linear rhythms established in Islamic art. An artist of the Dionysius circle, perhaps one of his sons, painted the remarkable icon *St Florus and St Lavrus* (popular patron saints of horses) (Plate 10). The grouping and stylized rendering of the horses here is quite oriental, resembling Persian miniatures of that

IV. (*facing*) VIRGIN AND CHILD (*above*). Moscow School, late 17th or early 18th century. The coats of arms were probably added later by an owner's family. VIRGIN OF THE SIGN (*below*), with elaborate design of small river pearls and precious stones in silver setting. Early 18th century.

time. This strange movement away from strict Byzantine towards the ornamental art of non-Christian Eastern neighbours became a striking feature of the later Stroganov school. It also characterized elaborately decorative icons of the late sixteenth- and early seventeenth-century Yaroslavl school (Plate 11).

The Turks finally captured Constantinople in 1453. And, throughout the following century, Moscow, as capital of the resurgent Russian State, but also self-styled spiritual heir of the fallen Byzantine Empire, became a new magnet, attracting artists both from provincial Russian centres and from conquered Greece. Hence the formation of something like a national style, common to all Russian icon painting, derived from the Muscovite absorption of local variants, began during this period. But it was accompanied by so many new techniques and divergent manners, introduced by migrant foreign artists, that it soon led to a bewildering outburst of eclecticism.

It none the less brought an influx of fresh vigour from abroad, clearly reflected even in the provincial schools. *The Resurrection* (Pskov School, sixteenth century) depicts a dynamic full-bodied Christ, surging upwards out of hell, against an aureole of light, surrounded by angels, cherubim, and seraphim. Underneath him hell is represented in the traditional way as a prison with serrated walls (Plate 12). The portable Iconostasis (Moscow or Novgorod School, sixteenth century), (Plate 16), though its elongated swaying saints and angels are typical of Novgorod, is far stronger, more varied and compact in grouping than the earlier work of Dionysius and his circle. The figures of the saints are bowed in silent prayer, while those of prophets are animated and eloquent. All are united by a graceful rhythm.

Our Lady of the Burning Bush (Pskov School, late fifteenth century) represents one of the most complex Byzantine themes, treated here with strongly geometrical definition and purity of style. The Virgin Mary and the infant Christ are set in a circle, intersected by eight triangular segments, painted with gospel symbols and angels (Plate 13).

At the same time another, more distinctly individual, school of icon painting emerged through the patronage of the Stroganov family, adventurous merchant princes who, with the aid of hardy Don Cossacks, were carrying out the commercial conquest and colonization of Siberia. Emigrating eastward from Novgorod, this energetic and cultured family acquired immense tracts of land, where they built whole new towns, like Solvychegodsk, which became a thriving centre for fine sacred silver and enamel work. The Stroganovs seem to have developed a discriminating taste for all the arts, and engaged numerous painters to make for them beautiful and elaborate house icons. Though they inherited from fifteenth-century Novgorod its attenuated physical proportions – long bodies with small heads – and mannered grace of gesture, the Stroganov painters specialized in gorgeous colours and oriental miniature scenes, glowing against rich gold backgrounds.

The art historian, D. Rovinsky, unearthed the names of several painters who worked for the Stroganovs in the late sixteenth and early seventeenth century, after which many of them were drawn into the Tsar's painting workshops in Moscow. Procopius Chirin (second half of the seventeenth century) is known to have received commissions from the Stroganov family, but later became a salaried painter for the Tsar. He developed a talent for pure jewel-like colours and for laying on liquid gold with a brush, to render fluid patterns in some rich brocade. The Stroganovs were ardent collectors of *objets d'art*, renowned for their love of splendid Persian and Indian materials, jewellery and illuminated manuscripts. The school of icon painting which arose from their patronage gave scope to their own exotic taste and personal interest in more individual portraiture. It never became a slavish copy of the Persian miniature style.

But it reflected a time when Russian art could afford to become more receptive to Asiatic culture, since her former Tartar oppressors had been transformed into submissive subjects. And Procopius Chirin, apart from his oriental decorative finesse, knew how to impart a strain of Christian mysticism to the faces of his saints, as they gaze upwards and fix their eyes on Christ or on some holy vision (Plates 14 and 15).

In Moscow plans for building a grand new Kremlin of churches and palaces started to materialize in the second half of the fifteenth century. The Uspensky Cathedral was built in 1479, that of the Annunciation was rebuilt in 1485, and the Archangel Cathedral was started in 1505. In 1547 the Tsar established a school for icon painters and central workshops (later attached to the State Armoury) employing permanent salaried craftsmen. They worked solely for the Tsar and for the embellishment and maintenance of the Moscow cathedrals. Icons began to grow more narrative in subject-matter and more elaborately magnificent in style. A sort of vigorous Byzantine baroque animated and drew together the arts of painting, precious metalwork, coloured enamel and jewelled settings. The heads of the holy figures became adorned with crowns or haloes, and their necks with

V. ST FLORUS AND ST LAVRUS, with St George and a Patriarch. Probably St Petersburg School, late 18th century.

repoussé gold or silver-gilt collars, enamelled in glowing colours or engraved with nielloed arabesques, and often encrusted with precious stones and pearls (Plate 17).

The Great Fire of 1547 destroyed or damaged many churches and works of art in Moscow. It impelled Ivan the Terrible, who had just taken full power, to start his *royal workshops*, and to invite more than three hundred German, Italian, and other foreign painters, sculptors, jewellers, and craftsmen, to come to work in Russia. Apart from the dominant note of regal semi-oriental splendour pervading the new 'national' style, the influx of West European artists and engravings brought new familiarity with the full-bodied Renaissance manner of depicting the human form, a stronger sense of physical substance and of the more complicated human moods and passions. The already sickly spirituality and stereotyped ritual poses of many standard fifteenth-century icons could not resist that temptingly healthy and robust infusion.

Such a rare blend of vital foreign elements and determined royal encouragement ought to have enabled a large number of talented men to dedicate their lives to improving religious art. But in the matter of ruthless State exploitation of the whole available stock of spiritual forces, the organizers of these Moscow workshops showed themselves worthy precursors of Soviet officialdom. Already the Moscow Tsars urged their Embassies abroad to persuade good foreign craftsmen to take service in Moscow, and teach Russian apprentices there. The results often fell below expectation, because foreigners might prove reluctant to give away their cherished trade secrets to outsiders. But while foreign experts seem to have received reasonably good treatment in the capital, so long as their services were indispensable, native draughtsmen, painters, and restorers, from other parts of Russia, were simply conscripted and sent to work in Moscow. Their lot was hard, and often miserable. Ecclesiastical tutelage also harassed them by tyrannizing over their moral welfare. Poor bewildered craftsmen, forced to work in depressing squalor, were ordered to be humble and modest in character, never to indulge in quarrels or drunkenness, told that they must 'keep their souls pure' and live obediently under the supervision of their spiritual guides.

We do not know how far these formidable injunctions were taken seriously, but the creative initiative of these long-suffering men must have been damped by endless material pin-pricks, by unremittent bullying, and by such strange orders as: 'He that shall paint an icon from his own imagination shall suffer endless torment.' The latter indicates the growing concern of the Orthodox Church to promote and fortify what they regarded as religious (traditional) iconic forms rather than 'carnal' (independent Western) tendencies in figurative art.

The political upheavals of the *Time of Troubles* (1604–13) painfully interrupted the progress of religious art in Moscow. But it rapidly recovered and reached a new zenith in the reign of Tsar Alexei Mikhailovich (1645–76), himself an enthusiastic lover and patron of the arts. The time had come when moral servitude to Byzantium, physical fear of Tartar conquerors and the paralysing threats of civil war, had all receded. In the self-confident, though not yet chauvinistic, Moscow nation-state, royal ceremonial assumed a more luxurious character, while remaining strictly symbolic and linked with edifying religious ritual. The *Crucifixion*, illustrated in colour here (Plate II), with its gilded crucifix, pious but splendidly robed figures and palatial architectural background, is a good example of this period. The State Armoury had grown into a department for the production of gold and silver ornaments and regal icons (Plates 18 and 19). Yet alongside this majestic court art of the metropolis, there continued in the provinces pious and authentic but far simpler schools of icon painting, closer to the late Novgorod style and mode of composition (Plate 20).

The normally blighting effect of official control on art was obviated by a skilful choice of personnel. In 1654, Tsar Alexei Mikhailovich appointed as Director of the Armoury the Boyar Bogdan Hitrovo, a highly gifted and versatile nobleman, who had already distinguished himself in State service as a soldier, diplomat, judge, and administrator. Talent, creative skill, and zeal were infinitely more important to him in selecting artists, than their national origin and political or religious credentials. A motley mixture of Poles, Germans, Tartars, Armenians, Greeks, Jews, and Swedes, all seem to have worked amicably and fruitfully together under Hitrovo's supervision. He became a kind of seventeenth-century Diaghilev, imposing his discriminating discipline on the visual arts in Russia. While he never favoured thoughtless copying of the latest foreign models, he encouraged a thorough study of them, and believed that they could be blended with native interpretation to serve Russian artistic needs.

We know that in 1662 sixty foreign artists and craftsmen were working for the State Armoury. Many stayed on and became Russian citizens. Open and responsive to East and West alike, guided by a man with a strong sense of purpose and broad knowledge, the religious and elaborate decorative art of Moscow reached a high level at this time. Hitrovo was greatly helped in his task through receiving the constant support and confidence of the Tsar. He needed all the support he could get in coping with that puritanical zealot, the Patriarch Nikon, who, after 1652, headed the Church campaign against baleful Western influences, alleged to be undermining the robust Christian modesty of Russian art.

For Nikon the function of icons was merely to act as a visual aid in maintaining the impregnable power of Church doctrine over sinful humans. The more lively realistic 'Western' manner of painting icons, already prevalent in the seventeenth century, deeply disturbed the Church, who saw in it a weakening of their ascetic type of religious discipline. Paul of Aleppo, a visitor to Moscow at this time, was amazed at how little attention the crude priests paid to the artistic quality of icons. 'They pay no heed either to the beauty of the image or the skill of the painter. All icons are for them the same, whether beautiful or hideous—they revere them all equally and bow before them, even if the icon is only a sketch on paper or a child's rough drawing.'[1]

Thus Nikon supported the ancient manner of icon painting, and protested against the new, solely as a means of maintaining meek obedience to the Church. In a service which he held in 1655 in the Cathedral of the Dormition in the Kremlin, he condemned and excommunicated all who had painted icons in the Western manner, and anybody who should dare to keep such icons in their houses. He showed to the congregation icons which he had brought together and then threw them on the stone floor with such violence that they broke into fragments. He then ordered them to be burned in public. But the Tsar, who was present, gently suggested that it would be better to bury them in the ground, and this in fact was done.

On another occasion Nikon sent his men to take away all the icons painted in the Western or 'Frankish' style, even from the houses of high State officials. He then gave an order to pierce through the eyes of all the offending icons and have them carried through the city of Moscow, as a warning to heretical innovators. Nevertheless, for Avakum, and the Old Believers, even Nikon seemed half-hearted in resisting what they fanatically denounced as a devilish, pagan profanation of pure icon painting.

Avakum contended that pious painters committed a grievous sin if they ever

[1] N. Andreyev, 'Nikon and Avakum on Icon Painting', *Revue des Etudes Slaves*, Vol. 38, Paris, 1961.

depicted Christian saints as 'full-bodied and sensual', and not as thin, ascetic, and ethereal. He complained that saints were thus being turned into 'temptations of the Devil', that the icon of the Saviour, 'with a plump face, full red lips, and golden curls', was encouraged by the wicked Nikon, who followed the bad fashion set by profane Germans. He was horrified that 'the hair of the saints is combed' and that they were depicted 'after the manner of earthly things'.

If the humane ideal of a brighter, more inspiringly beautiful and spiritually animated religious art appealed to the Tsar and the Boyar B. Hitrovo, it was certainly anathema both to Nikon and Avakum. And it was not till after 1658 (when Nikon ceased to be Patriarch) that the major artistic innovations of Ushakov and his followers were given the chance to flourish. But by then the bitter quarrel about icon painting had been dragged as a weapon into the Great Schism. This helps us to understand how the decisive break in Russian culture started, not in the later reign of the revolutionary Peter the Great, but already in that of the pious and gentle Alexei Mikhailovich.

The indomitable Hitrovo, however, not only refused to be swayed by any official priestly xenophobia, but in 1664 he appointed Simon Ushakov (1626–86) to be head of his department for icon painting. Ushakov is justly famous, both for his new blend of human and divine elements in religious art, and for the decisive manner in which he turned to the West for inspiration. The serene but lifelike figures of Christ, in which he excelled, show features neither too dry, emaciated or detached from this earthly world, nor too carnally human and meticulously prosaic. They are noble physical figures, who undergo spiritual suffering and pain, but in which the spirit, without violent strain or ostentation, quietly triumphs over the flesh. Although devoid of any obvious *national* character (for they might equally well be Greek, Russian or Italian), Ushakov's Christian images reflect the compelling originality of a profoundly gifted and independent-minded artist.

His *Icon of the Vernicle*, painted in 1673 (Plate 21), is a highly successful attempt to infuse life into the stereotyped Orthodox image of Christ, by endowing it with the latest refinements of an understood and adapted European technique. In so doing, Ushakov in no way realistically debased the symbolic Orthodox type, but gave richer, softer contour, roundness and personal character to every part of the Saviour's face. While he got rid of hard and dull iconographic rigidity, especially in his treatment of the nose, eyes, and mouth, he maintained the serene purity of the icon style and its prime concern with inward spiritual expression. His

VI. THE ROSTOV MIRACLE WORKERS.
Painted on copper in enamel colours.
Second half of 18th century.

pictures of *The Virgin and Child* reveal exactly the same approach, and solve the problem almost equally well (Plate 22).

Clearly Ushakov was on the right track, when he boldly sought guidance from the West, instead of going back, as the savage reforming priests demanded, to copy old Greek models more meticulously. Only he was badly served by his less gifted disciples, who tried to follow his freer and subtler representational style, but lacked the trained observation, draughtsmanship and power of interpretation, required to achieve mastery in it. The familiar type of *Russian Saviour*, so frequently copied from Ushakov, lacks majesty and is often devoid of positive character. Once the divine face had lost its strong severity and sensitive contours, it sank too easily into a new convention of vapid goodwill or sentimental Italianate prettiness. But this was not an inevitable failing, for some of Ushakov's disciples and contemporaries painted almost as well as he did, and in a similar style (Plate 23).

It is none the less remarkable that certain iconographic types seem to have remained almost unaffected by the Western mode of painting. Icons of St John the Baptist, for instance, are faithful to the prototype of the hermit, dressed in a shaggy camel's hair coat, with bony arms and legs like sticks, and concentrated eyes that convey a look of ecstasy. This strong-willed ascetic, who could renounce all human temptations and fast in the desert, was a favourite type, both in Byzantine and Russian art, where he also figured as *St John with the Wings*, the one who announced the coming of the Saviour, and held on his breast a vessel containing the naked Child Jesus. Moreover, St John was not only familiar to Russians as a prophet and exemplary character, but still more as the patron saint of endless Russian *Ivans* (Plate 24).

Towards the end of the seventeenth century icon painting grew more deliberately illustrative and literary, with a predilection for complicated subjects, such as *The Creed, The Second Coming of Christ, the Festivals of the Church*, etc. Overloaded narrative compositions strained the resources of iconic style by seeking to represent effectively on a single wooden panel such shattering events as storms and earthquakes, ominous signs in the sky, the destruction of Babylon, or the end of the world. In the same period there developed a taste for exquisite small-scale paintings of separate biblical scenes, set in rows from top to bottom, or across a single icon, and for versions of the Archangels Gabriel and Michael, based on pictures from the Italian Renaissance courts, where the most elegant male heads were covered with abundant golden curls.

The icon illustrated here in colour (Plate III) is a striking example of the dynamic sacred miniature, though, according to the authorities of the new German icon museum at Recklinghausen, it should not be dated earlier than the mid-eighteenth century. The centre panels depict the *Crucifixion, Resurrection* and *Descent into Hell* with an almost baroque vehemence and vibration. It is completely surrounded by miniature pictures of Church festivals. But more classical Byzantine versions of the Virgin and Child could still be beautifully painted. In many seventeenth-century icons the face, hands, and drapery are treated with all the Western fullness and sensitive *finesse*, mastered and insisted on by Ushakov. This trend continued in the early eighteenth century, though more attention was then paid to decorative silver and vestment set with jewels and river pearls, but without detracting from the religious serenity of the central subject (Plate IV).

The close of the seventeenth century is often referred to by purists as the end of the history of icon painting proper, because it saw the withering of local Russian variants on Byzantine styles, and the triumphant adaptation of post-Renaissance West European modes of painting for sacred subjects. But we should remember that traditional styles continued to be honoured among the Old Believers, among whom were many rich merchant families, who lavishly patronized this form of art throughout the eighteenth and nineteenth centuries. Even Peter the Great, despite his withering contempt for the clergy, did not persecute icon painting as a craft, and he is known to have made gifts of icons, though many old church icons fell into wanton neglect and disrepair during his reign. But the spiritual reaction, which quickly started against Peter's prosaic technological drive, only intensified the prime importance still attached by a zealous minority to maintaining mystic imagery as a solace and refuge for the faithful.

As N. Kondakov clearly pointed out in his polemic with the purist critic, P. Muratov, it is wholly wrong to claim that on the threshold of the eighteenth century Russian religious art was relapsing into an infantile condition. On the contrary, lavish orders for family icons, and as gifts to monasteries, continued unabated; while icons acquired in the reign of Catherine the Great and her grandson, Alexander I, the more luxurious and polished secular brilliance of that age, they rarely lost their Christian sincerity (Plates 25 and 26). The icon of the gorgeously attired SS Florus, Lavrus, and George, shown here in colour (Plate V), with all its decorative realism, still maintains Byzantine formality in grouping and a sense of devotional rapture in the faces. The magnificent painted enamel of the *Rostov*

VIIA. ST NICHOLAS THE
MIRACLE WORKER. South
Russian School, early 19th
century.

VIIB. ST CATHERINE THE
MARTYR. Late 18th or early
19th century.

Miracle Workers, from the same period, is even richer and more brilliant in subtle polychrome colouring, but preserves a truly iconic serenity despite its elaborate pyramidal composition of grouped figures (Plate VI).

The most important orders for painting in the new Petersburg cathedrals were given to leading Court artists, like V. Borovikovsky, who were already masters of the secular Western style of portraiture, but none the less loved religious painting. The favourite Russian saints and martyrs, St Nicolas the Miracle Worker, St George, SS Boris and Gleb, St Catherine the Martyr, continued to be painted throughout the Empire, though with increasing freedom from former iconographic convention and fewer local variants (Plate VII). And in the depths of the country religious art survived in the manner of a special peasant craft, notably in certain village districts, where the best wood was grown for making seasoned panels, and where groups of local craftsmen had for long been accustomed to work co-operatively, as in Mstera, Palekh, and Kholuy.

During the nineteenth century many of these village painters, struggling to keep themselves in regular paid employment, reluctantly accepted orders to supply large numbers of cheap icons, especially those intended to be covered with metallic repoussé surrounds, for which only the exposed faces, hands, and feet needed to be hand-painted. Finally the enterprising manufacturers of tin boxes, and commercial containers, were tempted by the profitable prospects of printing mass-produced icons on tin plate. They opened factories for this purpose, for which, it must be noted, they received the full approval of the grossly philistine *Holy Synod*. The quality of these colour prints was even fairly good, though stamped with uniformity by a mechanical process (Plate 27B). When the unfortunate icon-painting villages appealed to the Holy Synod for protection of their cherished craft, the Government appointed a committee to draw up a report. The latter made the rather futile recommendation that the artistic standard of these village crafts-men should be improved by more systematic school instruction in draughtsman-ship and iconography. Another turning-point where a golden opportunity was missed! It is sad that the historical and archaeological interest in icons, which revived so strongly in Russia throughout the nineteenth century, did nothing energetic, either to find wider scope for the creative talent of contemporary village artists or to improve the erratic taste of their would-be patrons.

On the contrary, cheap, gaudy and garish icons, encased in plain brass or white metal surrounds, were mass produced for peasant and shopkeeper homes.

The factories simply bought up icons still painted by the villagers of Mstera or Palekh, and then sold colour-printed reproductions at a lower price than the hand-painted originals. And the peasants became content to hang these prints on the wall in the *red corners* of their huts. Some wealthier families still commissioned fine hand-painted icons for their name-days, homes or churches, but not enough to keep the poor artists from preferring factory work, to provide them with a more regular livelihood. Then numerous brass icons were still made in provincial centres, some inlaid with coloured enamel, preserving excellent and original craftsmanship right up to the end of the nineteenth century (Plate 27A).

Meanwhile, however, one important new outlet had been found, which partly compensated for the doom of icon painting as an art. Enlightened men of affairs, already in the eighteenth century, started practical attempts to divert the inherited skill of local craftsmen into the painting of secular subjects on lacquered boxes and decorative objects of utility (see Chapter Seven). After the Revolution, the Soviet Government resumed this policy, which still prevails.

1. THE VIRGIN OF VLADIMIR. Brought from Constantinople to Kiev in the early 12th century. A revered prototype, copied countless times by Russian icon painters. *Tretyakov Gallery, Moscow.*

2. HEAD OF AN ANGEL. Fragment of a fresco from the Dmitrievsky Cathedral at Vladimir. 12th century.

3. THE APOSTLES ST PETER AND ST PAUL. From the Saint Sophia Cathedral,
Novgorod. Probably Byzantine. 12th century. *Novgorod Museum*.

4. THE VIRGIN OF THE SIGN. The infant Christ, represented in a medallion on his mother's breast, repeats her gesture of intercession. Yaroslavl School, 13th century.
Tretyakov Gallery, Moscow.

5. ST JOHN THE EVANGELIST WITH ST GEORGE AND ST BLAISE.
Novgorod School, 13th century. *Russian Museum, Leningrad.*

6. THE VIRGIN MARY. Theophanes the Greek, 1405. Detail from an icon in the Cathedral of the Annunciation, Moscow.

7. NOAH. Theophanes the Greek, 1378. Fresco in Church of
the Transfiguration, Novgorod.

8. Frescoes on portal of Church of the Virgin's Birth, Therapont Monastery. Dionysius, between 1500 and 1502.

9. THE ASCENSION. Novgorod or Moscow School, second quarter of 15th century. *Tretyakov Gallery*.

10. ST FLORUS AND ST LAVRUS (popular patron saints of horses). Late 15th century.
Tretyakov Gallery.

11. THE OLD TESTAMENT TRINITY. Yaroslavl School, *c.* 1600. *By courtesy of the Walters Art Gallery, Baltimore, U.S.A.*

12. THE RESURRECTION. Pskov School, 16th century. Former collection of the brothers Chirikov, Moscow.

13. OUR LADY OF THE BURNING BUSH. Pskov School, late 15th century. Former collection of
S. Ryabushinsky, Moscow.

14. ST JOHN THE BAPTIST. Stroganov School, early 17th century.

15. ST JOHN THE WARRIOR. Procopius Chirin. Stroganov School, early 17th century. Former collection of N. Likhachev, Petersburg.

16. PORTABLE ICONOSTASIS. School of Novgorod or Moscow, mid-16th century. Recorded in *Thirty-five Russian Primitives*, by P. Muratov, 1931. *By courtesy of 'A la Vieille Russie', New York.*

17. THE ARCHANGEL GABRIEL SURROUNDED BY ANGELS (detail). Painted by order of Ivan the Terrible for the Cathedral of the Annunciation, Moscow. Late 16th century.

18. VIRGIN AND CHILD. Moscow School, early 17th century. *Private collection, London*.

19. VIRGIN OF VLADIMIR. Moscow School, 16th century. The magnificent setting, chased in gold with
floral sprays in enamel and precious stones, was added in the early 17th century.
By courtesy of 'A la Vieille Russie', New York.

20. THE CRUCIFIXION. Northern Russian School, 17th century.
Private collection, London.

21. ICON OF THE VERNICLE. Simon Ushakov, 1673. *Trinity Sergius Monastery, Moscow.*

22. VIRGIN AND CHILD. Simon Ushakov, later half of 17th century.

23. CHRIST ENTHRONED. Nikita Pavlov (a contemporary of Ushakov), mid-17th century.
Cathedral of Novodevichy Convent, Moscow.

24. ST JOHN WITH THE WINGS, holding a vessel with the infant Jesus. Early 17th century.
The enamelled *riza* is a 19th century addition.

25. THE DEAD CHRIST WITH THE VIRGIN MARY AND ST JOHN. Northern Russian School,
18th century. Set in exceptionally well-designed 19th century silver-gilt surround, with embossed
haloes and foliage.

26. *(left)* CROWNED VIRGIN AND CHILD, with elaborate nielloed silver surround. Dated 1795. *(right)* Icon painted with scenes from the life of the Virgin. 17th century. *Collection, Mrs May, Washington, D.C.*

27B. ST PANTELEIMON. Colour print on tin foil: this technique for mass production marked the end of icon painting as a fine art. Last decade of 19th century.

27A. DORMITION OF THE VIRGIN. Icon in brass and coloured enamel: time-honoured theme repeated in a cheap material, while retaining high level of style and craftsmanship. Mid-19th century.

CHAPTER TWO

Religious and Secular Silver, and Artistic Work in Precious Metals

The knowledge and artistic repute of Russian work in precious metals have suffered for long from the scanty interest shown in them by many Westernized Russians and by most Europeans. This neglect has recently been overcorrected by an effort to demonstrate unique gifts and dazzling national originality, peculiar to Russians. In fact, the best Russian metalwork assimilated a bewildering variety of features, derived both from East and West, though more from the latter (if we include Byzantium as a survival from the Roman Empire) and foreign artists of diverse nationalities played a prominent part in its creation from the earliest times. But it is an art to which Russia made a major contribution.

That tiresome and artificial dispute, playing on national vanity, as to whether foreign or native craftsmen, imported fashions or national tradition, led the way, dwindles in importance through unmistakable visual evidence that many talented foreigners worked in a different manner when they were employed in Russia, and that they taught Russian pupils (who might surpass their masters). In any case these foreigners did more to stimulate than to impede the growth of characteristic styles and technique on Russian soil.

The French architectural and art historian, Viollet-le-Duc, likened Russia to a vast laboratory, where the art of contrasting races clashed and mingled in the formation of a strange hybrid, mediating between Asia and the West. Exuberant be-jewelled splendour from northern India, or learned from Sassanian Persia, curly calligraphic and geometrical motifs from Islam, the naïve wooden crafts of a nearly static Slav peasantry, combined with a sternly ascetic Byzantine strain, and with newer, more refined secular tastes, derived from Italy, Germany, and France, and already established in seventeenth-century Russia.

Three of the most typical and striking genres, brought to a new high point in Russian precious-metal work, had, of course, flourished previously in the multi-

VIII. Imperial Orb in gold set with precious stones, with sacred scenes painted in enamel colours. Made for the first Romanov Tsar, Michael, early 17th century.

national Byzantine Empire, namely niello, filigree, and patterns in coloured enamel. Niello, executed in the manner it acquired in Russia, demanded an expert draughtsman as well as a master engraver. For the design was first drawn upon the silver surface, then chased, in order to lower the pattern, after which the hollowed sections were filled with a black enamel alloy. Then the article was heated in the kiln until the enamel fused with the silver. Finally a workman polished it, until the pure black linear design or decorative lettering became flush with the surface of the silver background.

Filigree, the art of making intricate lacy patterns out of malleable gold or silver wire, was known from ancient times in Russia as *skan*. It figured prominently in adorning the covers of sacred books or the surrounds of icons, and the silver wire was skilfully soldered against a solid silver background. Nineteenth- and twentieth-century excavations from burial mounds and sites of ruined towns have also brought to light many early filigree ornaments dating from the ninth to the thirteenth centuries. The Russian style of filigree developed a strikingly compact geometrical composition of spiral scrolls, merging in a rhythmic flow against smooth or embossed surfaces (Plate 28).

Many Greek enamellers came to work in Kiev prior to the Mongol invasion. But the iconographic expert, N. Kondakov, maintained that in the eleventh and twelfth centuries Russian enamellers on precious metals under the Kiev Grand Princes produced work as fine as that of the most talented Byzantine Greeks. He proved that a princely diadem, excavated in 1889, had *not* been made by Greeks, because it revealed obvious ignorance in rendering detail of classical drapery on the enamelled figures, and because it introduced a turquoise blue pigment, unknown in Byzantium.

The destructive lust of Mongol hordes who overran and occupied the greater part of Russia in the mid-thirteenth century obliterated nearly all the gold and silver vessels, which were easily looted, broken and melted down. In Kiev alone hundreds of churches were left as smoking ruins by the Mongols. But after the sack of Kiev the centre of fine silver craftsmanship shifted to Novgorod, which escaped the Mongols, and where many skilled artists continued to work peacefully for the monasteries and churches until the end of the fifteenth century, when Novgorod was sacked and annexed by its compatriots from resurgent Moscow. The silver work of Novgorod, and of Kostroma, another local centre, tends to be cruder and more provincial than that of earlier Kiev or later Moscow, but some first-class specimens, both of sacred and secular silver, have survived (Plate 29).

Novgorod's close trade relations with the Hanseatic towns attracted North German artists to work in Russia, where their talents appear to have received fresh scope. This may explain the origin of a crystal barrel in a fantastic silver-gilt setting, presented by the Metropolitan of Novgorod to the Tsar Ivan III when he annexed that city in 1478. This exuberantly pagan work illustrates the territorial extent and power of Renaissance influence in northern Europe in the fifteenth century. The sides of the mount are chased with Bacchanalian scenes, and a nude young Bacchus sits on the lid, pouring wine into a beaker (Plate 30).

Integrated Moscow gradually conquered its moral servitude to copying Byzantine models, and overcame the old paralyzing fear of cunning Tartar rulers, though it took two centuries to shake off the Tartar yoke. That healthier more self-confident Russian state of mind led to a vigorous upsurge of decorative art in the sixteenth century. Foreign envoys who visited Russia at this time bore witness to the dazzling splendour and abundance of gold and silver vessels, encrusted with precious stones as large as nuts. These, and the jewelled majesty of the Tsar himself, overawed foreign guests at royal receptions and feasts in the Moscow palaces. The Church became equally lavish in ordering or acquiring sumptuous objects to render its own ceremonial more impressive and alluring and hold its audience spellbound. Unfortunately much of this gorgeous sixteenth-century work was in its turn destroyed during the chaotic Time of Troubles in the early seventeenth century.

After the Poles had been driven out of Moscow, the more stable rule of the early Romanov Tsars enabled Russian work in precious metals to reach another peak of mastery and a distinct kind of international originality (Plate VIII). Within the recently consolidated Empire, artists of many races, and skilled in all techniques, flocked to the new capital. But the Moscow Tsars (long before Peter the Great) also invited silversmiths from Holland, Germany, and England, and even from India and Persia.

One striking feature of early seventeenth-century Russian silver is the perfect chasing of finely stylized foliage and flowers in all-over patterns, which became thicker and more complex as the century proceeded (Plates 31, 32). Filigree was no longer plainly soldered on sheets of metal, but was filled with polychrome enamels, in which white, blue, and yellow shades predominated. Towards the end of the century this geometrical cloisonné enamel began to yield place to free miniature

IX. Crown of the Empress Anna Ioanovna. Gold, set with
diamonds and rubies, *c.* 1730.

portrait painting in enamel colours, a genre which reached its high point in the eighteenth century (Plate X).

Simultaneously, some provincial towns also began to flourish in the arts. Solvychegodsk, founded by that great merchant family, the Stroganovs, the commercial conquerors of Siberia, produced superb examples of free painting in enamel colours direct on silver surfaces (Plate X). The Stroganovs had a highly civilized sense of duty, for they educated their new town by buying serious works of art and acquiring for it exemplary specimens of silver from abroad. They appear to have encouraged Ukrainian artists, who painted silver bowls and boxes with peasant scenes, luxuriant and luscious foliage, huge tulips, garlands of sunflowers and daisies, and also with bold drawings of swans, turkeys, lions and stags (Plate 41).

Ceremonial dishes played an important part in the marriage ceremonies of old Russia. A grandiose specimen (Plate 33), dating from 1561, has survived in the *Oruzheinaya Palata* of the Moscow Kremlin. Its interior is chased with a simple but dynamic design of curved concave spirals, radiating from a central double-headed eagle, engraved in niello. The flat rim is adorned with a fine network of stylized foliage, varied by an old Slavonic inscription. Just as in ancient China, certain forms in jade or porcelain became revered as classical standards of supreme beauty, repeated with slight variations from one century to another, so did silversmiths in Russia repeat the refined simplicity of this circular dish, its interior curves and flat nielloed rim, right up to the early eighteenth century, when more sophisticated Western motifs prevailed.

Unique gold and silver vessels were highly cherished by their owners and seldom sold for profit. They changed ownership chiefly by inheritance. The grandest ones passed as gifts from Tsar to Patriarch, or as awards to deserving Boyars and other outstanding citizens. Sometimes from a disgraced Boyar, whose property had been confiscated, they would find their way back into the Imperial Treasury. Or, after the death of a wicked but conscience-stricken owner, they would be bequeathed to some monastery, there to promote the repose of his sinful soul.

Two traditional vessels, the *kovsch* and the *bratina*, derived from earlier models made in wood by Slav peasants, had boldly characteristic shapes. These differed from any metalwork made outside Russia. The *kovsch* was originally a low boat-shaped drinking-vessel, with a raised handle, like a ladle, used chiefly at feasts for drinking mead, *kvass* or beer (Plate 36). Gradually it lost its practical function, and turned into a symbol of honour for some important service to the State. It could be an award for a military feat, or for the successful conclusion of some diplomatic or commercial mission (Plate 37). For a long time its shape retained the same severe simplicity. Then, during the eighteenth century, Western fashions made it more ornate and complex. The late nineteenth century brought a fresh reaction in taste, which, led by Fabergé and other eminent silversmiths, produced fine ceremonial *kovschy*, but inspired by early seventeenth-century styles (Plate 38, Plate X).

The *bratina*, a loving-cup without handles, was always globular in shape, with a flat bandlike lip, usually inscribed with stylized Slavonic lettering (Plates 35A, 35B). When a royal prince died a favourite *bratina* of his was often placed in a church, where it could afterwards be consecrated for religious use as an incense-burner. A *bratina* which had originally belonged to Tsar Michael, the first Romanov, bears an inscription that it was placed on the coffin of the Tsarevich Ivan Ivanovich, to commemorate the murder of that prince by his father (Ivan the Terrible). Though the inscription round the rim sometimes records the name of the owner, or the purpose of dedication, it is often confined to a simple toast, or edifying maxim, such as: 'True love is a golden cup, which can never be broken; the soul alone can change it.'

Many persons of high rank had their own *bratina* made for them, and a few notable early specimens have survived. A most elaborate one, made for Peter Tretyakov, a State official in the first quarter of the seventeenth century, is illustrated in *Antiquities of the Russian Empire* (1852). Its foot is supported by miniature human caryatids, who appear to uphold the bowl on their heads and outstretched hands. The surface of the bowl is richly embossed with arabesques of flowers and foliage and four heraldic plaques. It is also remarkable in having a coved cover, finishing in a long-stemmed silver flower, identical to the one used on Persian and Chinese perfume-sprinklers at that time. The instructive inscription round the rim reads: 'As arms are needed by the warrior in battle, as rain in time of drought, as drink to the thirsty, and as a sincere friend to console in time of misfortune and sorrow, so concord and friendship are demanded from all those who would drink from this cup.'

Russians are reputed to be great drinkers. But it should be recalled that old Russian drinking customs were embellished by a lot of edifying ritual, exemplified by the *bratina*. The man who proposed a toast had to stand with his head un-covered, empty the cup to its dregs, then turn it upside down over his head, so that all could see that he had emptied it, and thereby sincerely wished the health of the person he had toasted.

Though the Orthodox Church resembled puritanical Islam in frowning on sculpture in the round, as a concession to idol worship or human sensuality, it permitted carving and chasing in high relief. In this way silver ornament of many kinds, especially the surrounds of icons, allowed striking sculptural gifts to be developed, so long as they were consecrated by their primary religious motive. An excellent example is the lid from the sarcophagus of the Tsarevich Dmitri, made in 1630 by the chief Kremlin silversmith for the Archangel Cathedral in Moscow (Plate 34). In 1812, when Napoleon captured Moscow, the body of the sarcophagus disappeared, but the superb gilded lid with its life-size figure of the young prince, embossed in high relief, is now among the treasures of the *Oruzheinaya Palata* in the Moscow Kremlin. The head is modelled with a severe but sensitive fullness, and the whole silver background, partly granulated and partly smooth, is filled in with rich patterns of interlacing foliage.

Until the middle of the seventeenth century the masters of the gold and silver chambers served both Imperial orders and those of the powerful and wealthy Moscow Patriarchs. The latter employed a huge staff of artists, craftsmen, and jewellers, for making church adornments, mitres, crucifixes, censers, and gorgeous covers for Church books. But in the 1650s the ambitious Patriarch Nikon started his own independent workshop near the patriarchal palace. About the same time a brilliant and able nobleman, the Boyar Hitrovo, was appointed by the Tsar Alexei Mikhailovich to take charge of all the Kremlin gold and silver work, a post which he retained for over twenty years. For him individual talent outweighed every national or religious prejudice. Records prove that he employed a medley of Poles, Germans, Tartars, Greeks, Swedes, and Russians. This happy blend of gifted multi-racial artists, under wise direction, may account for the extremely high and varied quality of Russian silver work during that period. Much of its ornament already sprang from Italian Renaissance motifs, especially its treatment of foliage, figuring graceful main stems, with numerous symmetrical side-shoots. But the increasing representation of animals and birds probably derived from Persia, and the love of certain kinds of niello from intercourse with Greek artists in the monasteries of Mount Athos.

At the turn of the seventeenth century drinking-cups of western European design, and huge covered tankards, similar to those from Augsburg, began to be made more frequently in Russia. The early eighteenth century saw the start of Petersburg silver, which flourished in the hands of many foreign craftsmen imported by Peter the Great to work in his new capital. As had happened previously, artists from abroad created a new blend in response to their changed environment (Plate 40 and Plate IX). The Russian Government was just as strict about maintaining the purity of precious metals as it was in taking measures to safeguard against debasement of the currency. Though marking of silver vessels started in the seventeenth century, it remained erratic, and inscriptions are often a surer clue to dates. In 1700 Peter issued a decree, which first made marking universal and systematic. In 1714 he also allowed foreign craftsmen in precious metals to form their own separate guild. The majority were then from Germany, and their records were still kept in German. Swedes took second place, and a number came from Finland.

Catherine II gave the same guilds more comprehensive rules, in a decree issued in 1785. The guild consisted of masters, journeymen, and apprentices, as in the West. A 'master' had to have a 'masterpiece' of his work approved by connoisseurs, after serving not less than three years as a journeyman. In 1793 the guild of Russian craftsmen in Petersburg had forty-four masters, and that of foreign craftsmen fifty-nine. The number of masters rose to about one hundred and fifty at the beginning of the nineteenth century. They often had foreign pupils, but also many Russian ones. The native Russian craftsmen for long tended to specialize in religious work, crucifixes, lamps, gospel covers and surrounds for icons (Plate 42). A few outstanding *émigré* artists, like the Frenchman, Ador, who made exquisite jewelled boxes for Catherine II, did not belong to any guild, and managed very well without them. Fine gold boxes, with enamelled portrait medallions, continued to be made till the late nineteenth century (Plate 44).

The Swiss, J. Pauzié, who worked for Peter's daughter, the Empress Elisabeth, completely remodelled the Imperial crown, to 'modernize' it for Catherine's coronation. But tired of being bullied and cynically exploited, as he said, by many of his Russian patrons, he left Russia in 1764, to spend his remaining years in his calmer native land. During that period a large number of beautiful embossed tall cups and beakers in silver-gilt were ordered for the palaces and the nobility. Also superb chalices, iconostases and wrought silver gates were made for many monasteries

x. (*facing, top to bottom*) Nielloed silver-gilt pendant, painted with picture of St Nicolas the Miracle worker in enamel colours. Late 18th century. Enamelled silver box, painted inside with flowers and an amorous peasant scene. Solvychegodsk School, 17th century. Enamelled silver-gilt salt-cellar in shape of a throne. Ovchinikov, Moscow, late 19th century. Silver-gilt enamelled *kovsch*. Late 19th century.

and churches (Plates 43, 47, 48). And magnificent silver pieces, for household use, were created even in remote provincial towns (Plates 45, 46).

Towards the end of the eighteenth century, and more markedly in the first half of the nineteenth, there started a strong emotional reaction against conventionally classical, dry or stereotyped Western styles, and taste reverted to earlier, more exotic, models. Filigree, niello, and coloured enamels, often combined with seventeenth-century shapes, came into their own again (Plates 43, 47, 49, 50, 52A and B). By order of the energetic Nicolas I, the Imperial Academy of Arts was compelled to undertake the first large-scale attempt to catalogue and illustrate widely scattered and hitherto little-known or appreciated masterpieces of Russian decorative art and icons, preserved in many places throughout the Empire.

The result emerged in the massive illustrated volumes *Antiquities of the Russian Empire* (1852), which are still the best records available, though many of the treasures have since vanished in the chaos of revolution and civil war.

Nicolas I also deserves credit for having the State Armoury in the Kremlin completely renovated and considerably enlarged, so that the Imperial collection of gold and silver vessels and Crown jewels could be transferred there, and displayed to the maximum advantage. In recent years the Soviet authorities have added to it, and reopened it to the public.

In the second half of the nineteenth century, while the range of objects which they made was widening, the best Russian silversmiths returned increasingly for inspiration to Byzantine Muscovite motifs, to more grandiose and massive shapes, and to a revival of the ancient techniques of filigree, niello, and brilliantly coloured enamels (Plates X, XI). The latter became a speciality of the leading Moscow jewellers and silversmiths, Ovchinikov, Khlebnikov, and Lyubavin. But it was also pursued by the far better-known Fabergé, Sazykov, and Morozov in Petersburg.

Two pieces made by Sazykov between 1856 and 1864 (Plate 51A) illustrate the revival of the older oriental strains in decorative silver. The massive coffee-pot and wine-jug made in the same period (Plates 57, 58) show how effectively the old Slavonic type of ornament could be adapted to contemporary objects of utility. The richly enamelled but dignified teapot and wine-goblets (Plate 54) are good examples of slightly later work from the Moscow silversmith, Khlebnikov. The small cigarette box (on the same plate) reveals the exquisite painting of miniature peasant scenes on red lacquered silver, another speciality of that period.

Several good silversmiths made fine cups and saucers, as well as cigarette-cases and snuff-boxes, with delicately incised or nielloed architectural scenes, and land-scapes with human figures (Plates 49, 50, 56). These carried on, with individual variations, a sound tradition established in the late eighteenth and early nineteenth centuries. Certain domestic utensils, like teapots and trays, achieved an attractive fusion of modern European and Muscovite Russian styles (Plate 59), whereas objects like silver glass-holders for tea retained a uniquely Russian character right up to the early twentieth century (Plate 53). In many products semi-oriental, old Slav, and modern European styles, continued almost side by side. A beautifully engraved but Sassanian-looking pot could be made by Moscow silversmiths, at nearly the same time as a typically European tall cup and cover, decorated with a characteristic Russian prancing *troika* (Plates 55, 60).

Space does not permit me to do justice to the master silversmith and jeweller, Carl Fabergé, whose unique work, while justly famous, has been allowed to over-shadow the achievements of other less-known but first-class Russian silversmiths and jewellers. His fantastic Easter Eggs, made for the Imperial Family, his fanciful elaboration in *bijouterie* of classical French motifs, have already been fully de-scribed and documented by specialists. But we are apt to forget that Fabergé also drew from old Muscovite Byzantine tradition that fresh touch of pungent Russian idiom, that stimulating *genius loci*, which exerted such a powerful spell over the best foreign artists who worked in Russia.

And some neo-Russian creations of Fabergé display a classical restraint which is absent from the flamboyant extravaganza of late seventeenth-century Russian silver. The small *kovsch* illustrated here (Plate 38) is an instructive example of this brilliant Fabergé adaptation. So, too, is the elegant tea-caddy (Plate XII), which blends in subdued tones old Slav folk-lore motifs, filigree spirals, and massive bosses. Fabergé also made delightfully shaped silver tea-services of a strictly contemporary simplicity, and luxuriantly enamelled spoons, inspired by Russian peasant art (Plates 61B, 62).

This highly individual renaissance of decorative art in late nineteenth-century Russia is a remarkable phenomenon. It becomes more understandable when one considers how western European taste, on which Russia confidently depended for so long, was then being shaken and eroded by waves of convulsive revivals, and though still skilfully eclectic, had grown wavering and erratic, losing its faith and firm foundation.

XI. (*above*) Silver cigarette box with Imperial double-headed eagle in coloured cloisonné enamel. (*below*) Silver-gilt cigarette box with cloisonné enamel decoration in Persian carpet style. Both late 19th century.

Comparing it now with contemporary western European work, the best Russian silver work seems to have preserved more integrity, grandeur of design and finesse of craftsmanship (Plate X). Indeed, it approximated to eighteenth-century European standards, which, in Europe itself, more rapidly disintegrated in a fluid modern technological society. This rare specimen of Russian *chinoiserie* (Plate XIV), conceivable in eighteenth-century Europe, in the late nineteenth century could only have been made in Russia. Of course, there is immense unevenness in the quality of 'neo-Russian' craftsmanship, whether from Moscow or Petersburg silversmiths. While at its best it can be bold, brilliant, and sensitive, at its worst it is blatantly coarse, gaudy, heavy, and monotonous. But the best is better than has yet been widely recognized outside Russia, perhaps because it is so little seen or known there. A gorgeous enamelled silver-gilt beaker, by Ovchinikov, made in the 1870s, proves how vanishing techniques in art and imaginative folk-lore ornament could still be triumphantly revived in a coldly prosaic age of urban industry (Plate XIII).

Though systematic marking and control of objects made in precious metals first came into force in 1700, under Peter the Great, inscriptions and workmanship enable us to date earlier objects with approximate accuracy. The Russian silver standard is represented by the numerals 84, 88, or 91, which indicate the number of *zolotniks* of pure silver in ninety-six parts (equivalent in weight to one continental pound). The standards for gold are represented by the numerals 56, 72, and 92, indicating the proportion of pure gold to ninety-six *zolotniks*.

The four regulation marks stamped on Russian silver were as follows: the maker's initials (sometimes his full name); second, the coat-of-arms of the city where the silver was tested; third, the initials of the assayer (the latter were often followed by the full date); fourth, the figure showing the proportion of pure silver. The St Petersburg city mark started as a crowned double-headed eagle, until it was replaced in 1742 by the new city arms, two crossed anchors with a sceptre in the centre. The Moscow mark has a St George and Dragon in various versions. After 1896 the separate town marks were dropped, and a woman's head with a *kokoshnik* head-dress was adopted as a general hall-mark, both for gold and silver objects.

Owing to the vagaries of fashion, western interest in Russian artistic silver work and jewellery has so far been largely confined to the charming but by no means representative extravaganza of Carl Fabergé, the inventive court-jeweller of the late nineteenth and early twentieth centuries. In fact, as this chapter indicates, the Russian contribution to this branch of art was far more original, magnificent and widely varied.

Owing to the many foreign craftsmen of diverse nationalities, who came to work in Russia, styles and techniques imported from Byzantium, Persia and northern India, became assimilated, especially in producing precious objects for the Moscow Tsars and Patriarchs in the sixteenth and seventeenth centuries. From the mid-seventeenth century onwards, craftsmen from West Europe, Italy, France, Holland, Germany and Sweden, played a much bigger part, and secular objects increasingly took the place of sacred ones throughout the Petersburg period.

That extraordinary artistic renaissance which took place in nineteenth-century Russia, to which Fabergé contributed, embraced a much broader revival of Byzantine, old oriental and modern Europe styles, skilfully adapted to serve contemporary human needs, and to feed a starved imagination. Since a similar vital blend had been already manifest in seventeenth-century Moscow, it could also be described as neo-Russian.

28. Silver-gilt gospel cover, chased with sacred figures in bas-relief against smooth background, surrounded by filigree scrolls. *From the Kyrillo-Byelosersky Monastery, c.* 1534.

29. Silver-gilt Zion (casket for holding gifts or holy relics), embossed with figures of the four evangelists. Made for the Saint Sophia Cathedral, Novgorod. 14th century.

30. Crystal barrel in unique silver-gilt setting, presented by the Metropolitan of Novgorod to Tsar Ivan III, when he captured that city in 1578. Probably made in the 15th century by north German silversmiths.

31. Oval casket for holding consecrated bread or relics. The centre is carved in agate with a bas-relief of the Virgin and Child, and the reverse side depicts a scene, the Baptism of Christ, in nielloed silver. Mid-17th century. Formerly in Sacristy of the Holy Synod.

32. Gold plate of the Tsar Alexei Mikhailovich, decorated with rosettes, flowers and interlacing foliage in coloured enamel. The border is set with sixteen rubies. Mid-17th century.
Kremlin, Moscow.

33. Gold nielloed dish, made for the Empress Maria Temrukovna in 1561. *Kremlin, Moscow.*

34. Lid of silver sarcophagus of Prince Dmitri, made by the Moscow court silversmiths in 1630. *Kremlin, Moscow.*

36. Gold and jewelled *kovsch*, made for Tsar Michael Fyodorovich in 1618. *Kremlin, Moscow.*

facing page

35A. (*above*) Silver *bratina* of the Emperor Ivan IV (the Terrible). Second half of 16th century. *Kremlin, Moscow.*

35B. (*below*) *Bratina*, nielloed with scrolls and scenes of peasant life. Mid-19th century. *Private collection, London.*

38. Engraved *kovsch*, inspired by 17th century style, with austere body and elaborate handle. Fabergé, late 19th century.

facing page

37. Oval *kovsch* in massive silver. The centre of the chased double-headed eagle holds a repoussé bust of Peter the Great. The inscription tells that Peter presented this *kovsch* to a Muscovite nobleman, who had concluded a successful commercial mission to China. Dated 1709. *Collection, Eugène Lubovich, Paris.*

39. Silver-gilt cup and cover, decorated with repoussé busts and stylized foliage in filigree. Dated 1733.

40. Silver-gilt cup and cover, chased with scrolls against polished and
matted grounds, with repoussé busts of Peter the Great and his daughter,
Elisabeth. Dated 175 (last figure erased).

41. Silver dish, painted with large flowers in enamel colours. Mid-17th century.
Former collection, Prince M. Kurakin at Kosatskoe.

---

facing page

42. Silver-gilt gospel cover, set with oval enamel plaque of the Saviour blessing. Surrounded
by enamelled cherubs' heads, angels, plaques of the Passion, and larger plaques of the four
Evangelists in the corners. Dated 1729.

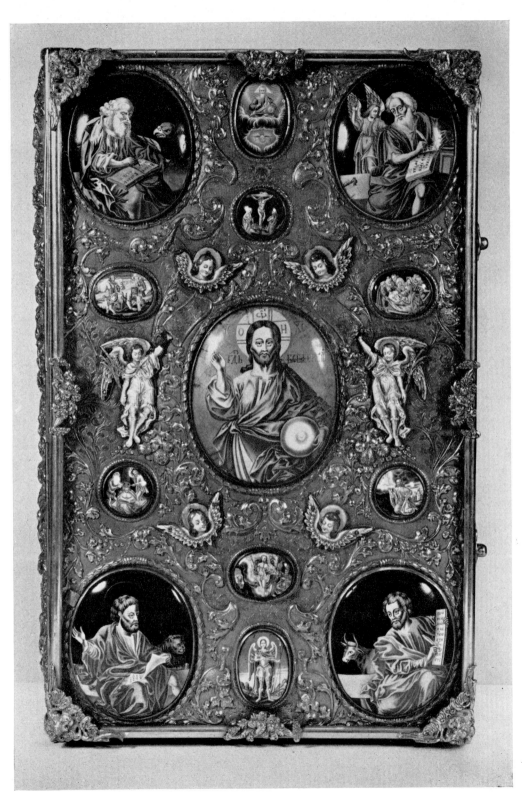

43. Silver-gilt altar-gates (*Royal Doors of the Priesthood*), presented by Catherine the
Great to the Kievo-Pecherskaya Lavra Monastery in 1784.
Collection, Mr Francis Stonor, London.

44. (*above*) Miniature of Princess Evgenia Yusupov, set in an elaborate frame, studded with rose diamonds. Late 18th century. Former Yusupov Collection. (*below, left*) Gold box painted with miniature of the Emperor Alexander I, probably by Isabey. Early 19th century. (*right*) Gold snuff-box, inset with oval miniature portrait of the Emperor Nicolas I. Petersburg, 1853.

Collection Mrs May, Washington, D.C.

45. Nielloed silver tea-caddy, made for a noble family, stamped with the town mark of Irkutsk.
Dated 1775.

46. Massive silver tankard, decorated with pastoral figures in niello. Moscow, 1800. (*behind*) Nielloed silver tray, engraved with coat of arms of the Sheremetyev family. Late 18th century. Other pieces from this service are in the Hermitage, Leningrad, and the State Historical Museum, Moscow.
Collection, Mrs May, Washington, D.C.

47. Display of 17th and 18th century Russian Church chalices. *Collection, Mrs May, Washington, D.C.*

48. Silver-gilt jewelled chalice, inset with coloured enamel plaques. 18th century.
Collection, Mrs May, Washington, D.C.

49. (*top*) Cigarette box, engraved with scene of an officer driving in a sledge. Early 19th century. (*centre*) Snuff-box, made to commemorate the marriage of Grand-Duke Paul and his second wife, Maria Fyodorovna. Late 18th century. (*bottom*) Box nielloed with landscape scene. Mid-19th century.

50. (*top left*) Box nielloed with scene of the Palace Square and Alexander Column, Petersburg. Early 19th century. (*top right*) Box nielloed with architectural scene. *c.* 1825. (*centre*) Box nielloed with view of Moscow Kremlin. *c.* 1850. (*bottom left*) Box with architectural scene bordered with baroque scrolls. Late 18th century. (*bottom right*) Box nielloed with scene depicting Falconet's statue of Peter the Great in Petersburg. Early 19th century.

52A. (*above*) Casket and glass-holder in silver filigree, reflecting traditional designs used for making Russian lace. Moscow, early 19th century.

52B. (*below*) Three beakers, illustrating changes of style in half a century. (*left*) With vigorous embossed heads and delicate foliage, Moscow, 1745. (*centre*) Engraved with birds, baroque scrolls and flowers, Moscow, 1771. (*right*) Nielloed with human figures and Cupids, Moscow, 1802.

facing page

51A. (*above, left*) Pieces illustrating mid-19th century revival of oriental styles. (*right*) Silver-gilt coffee-pot, engraved with Turkish motifs. Sazykov, 1864. (*left*) Covered jug with massive bosses and coiled dragon handle. Sazykov, 1856.

51B. (*below*) Casket, recumbent lion on cover and embossed border. Moscow, early 19th century.

53. Five glass-holders, illustrating variety of silver-ware made for this purpose throughout the 19th century. Some glasses are engraved to match their holders.

54. (*centre*) Silver-gilt teapot, chased with floral pattern in coloured cloisonné enamel, with boldly modelled spout. Khlebnikov, Moscow, mid-19th century. (*left and right*) Two chalice-shaped cloisonné enamel wine-cups. Moscow, *c.* 1870. (*below*) Painted silver cigarette box, *c.* 1870.

55. Covered pot engraved with human figures, wild animals and birds in Persian style. Moscow,
mid-19th century.

XII. Silver-gilt tea-caddy, decorated with bosses and 17th century folk-lore motifs in coloured enamel. Fabergé, late 19th century.

56. Silver-gilt cup and cover, engraved with geometrical designs and architectural scene in niello. Moscow, mid-19th century. *Private collection, London.*

57. Wine jug with cover, embossed in centre with a peasant figure driving a horse and harrow across a field. Probably made to celebrate the coronation of the Emperor Alexander II and his consort, whose heads are engraved on the base. Sazykov, 1856.

XIII. Silver-gilt beaker, enamelled with birds and stylised trees. Ovchinikov, late 19th century.

58. Massive engraved coffee-pot, inscribed round the rim. Sazykov, 1861.

59. Teapot, showing blend of Western shape with Russian type of spout and handle. Ovchinikov, Moscow, mid-19th century. (*background*) Hexagonal tray, chased foliage border. Gubkin, Moscow, 1841.

60. Cup and cover, high-relief *troika* applied in centre and gilded prancing horse on top. Petersburg, late 19th century.

61A. (*above*) Silver filigree fan. Mid-19th century.
61B. (*below*) Teapot and milk-jug, circular feet and handles. Fabergé, late 19th century.

XIV. Silver-gilt tea-caddy, brilliantly painted with *chinoiserie* scenes in enamel colours. Lyubavin, late 19th century.

62. Pair of silver serving spoons, pictures of ladies in ancient Russian costumes painted in enamel colours on the bowls. Fabergé, late 19th century.

The Birth of Russian Portrait Painting

The splendid decorative arts which served the Court, and all that stirring religious ritual, with which the semi-divine prestige of the Moscow Tsars were intimately linked, reached a grand climax in the seventeenth century. Then Peter the Great's decree of 1702 brought thousands of technical foreigners to work in his new capital. That ancient Russia of deeply resonant church bells, of solemn colourful processions led by bearded priests with icons, and sacred banners held aloft, of gay drunken popular festivals and haunting peasant songs, was temporarily abandoned by the stern command of Peter. Determined to transform his amorphous subjects into civilized and disciplined Europeans, Peter refused to be handicapped by any force of national pride or religious prejudice. Revered by his admirers as the Great Reformer, cursed by his enemies as the Tsar Anti-Christ, Peter none the less declared: 'I would rather have a stranger's son, but a good one, than my own, but a worthless creature!'

Before he called in a multitude of clever foreigners to teach his more receptive subjects the worldly Western sciences and arts, secular portrait painting in Russia, handicapped by dependence on religious iconography, was largely confined to formal *iconic* pictures of Tsars, Metropolitans, and Boyars (Plates 63, 64), showing them as heroic warriors, national leaders, or pure priest-kings. Peter, with characteristic thoroughness and care for beneficial change, encouraged the more substantial Western manner of portrait painting as a highly skilled craft, far less important to him than engineering or military science, yet providing a vital ingredient in the civilized hierarchical modern State which he desired to build.

He had himself, his wife and two daughters painted many times, and he believed that imposing, lifelike portraits of the leaders of society, placed in architectural or domestic settings worthy of their dignity, helped to stimulate respect and emulation from the lower ranks (Plate 65). Peter also sent a few native Russian artists to study in foreign countries. I. Nikitin (1690–1741) went to Italy and France, A. Matveyev (1701–39) to Holland. Both became proficient portrait

114

painters, and the former sometimes first-class. He painted several portraits of Peter and his second wife, later Catherine I. These have strikingly robust and solid qualities and display a mastery of European perspective and technique (Plate 65).

But Russian portrait painting in the early eighteenth century remained chiefly the work of migrant foreign artists, attracted into Russia by lavish Imperial patronage, and inspired to original efforts by their strange and fantastic new surroundings. The German ex-musician, turned roving portrait painter, Tannauer, came to Petersburg in 1709 (Plate 67), followed in 1714 by the Italian sculptor, K. Rastrelli, father of the famous architect, and a year later by the French painter, Louis Caravaque, from Marseilles. In the latter's contract with the Tsar, he undertook to paint portraits, battle scenes, flowers, animals, etc., for the Court, and also to teach Russian pupils the technique of contemporary oil painting. Though his contract bound him for three years only, he stayed in Russia till he died in 1754. One of his liveliest and most highly finished works is the double portrait of Peter's two young daughters, in the Romanov Gallery of the Winter Palace.

His best Russian pupil, who also studied under A. Matveyev, was the more famous A. Antropov (1716–95), son of a military carpenter of Ukrainian origin. Antropov proved the absurdity of the fashionable contention that a successful artistic career was then barred to men of humble origin. His astonishingly versatile talent was first employed in decorating the walls of Imperial palaces, but in 1752 he was sent to paint sacred scenes for the interior of the new St Andrew's Cathedral in Kiev (designed by the architect Rastrelli). After his return to the capital he began his maturest work and concentrated on portraits. These are powerful, personally expressive, compact, and often elegant, but free from the more trivial refinements and mannered gallicisms current in Elisabeth's reign. His portrait of Peter III, painted in 1762 (Plate 69), while it conveys the full regal majesty of ermine robes and lavish ornament, is far from formalizing or flattering Peter, who, with his tiny grotesque head and flabby limbs, looks like the vain and vicious weakling that he was. Antropov's portrait of Countess Apraksin (Plate 68) shows his robust talent at its masterly best.

Both F. Rokotov, the most gorgeously rococo of Russian painters (Plate 70), and the far greater D. Levitsky, studied for a time under Antropov. Thus the fruitful effect of foreign teachers on gifted Russian pupils became fully and very quickly manifest. Undeniably the discerning art-lover can trace here the subtle continuity and local enrichment of an imported Western style. Such periods of strong unbroken growth are rare in the explosive ups and downs of Russian culture, but no sensible Russian then felt ashamed to welcome beneficial foreign innovations.

Foreign artists were attracted to migrate to Russia, not only by a sense of rare adventure, but by the striking equality of opportunity offered by a country where the most enterprising of modern Emperors, a temporary dock labourer in Holland, had married a Livonian servant girl, who was even allowed to succeed him as the reigning Empress, Catherine I. Peter wrote frankly about her: 'Although the difference in our stations was great, I never regretted the choice I made, since, by marrying Catherine, I found myself possessed of an Empress, not only in name, but in reality, for her magnanimity and sound understanding.' A country so seemingly free from class prejudice, so democratic and flexible in accepting out-siders for their personal qualities and intrinsic ability, was bound to appeal to foreign artists, who longed for a broader scope and high rewards. Even when later they found themselves duped by illusory material expectations, they could still seek fulfilment in the imaginative realm of art, and on the whole found lavish patronage to back them.

But while Peter welcomed all qualified foreigners who had valuable skills, his light-hearted luxury-loving daughter, the Empress Elisabeth (who confessed she never knew that England was an island), decidedly preferred French artists, of whom de Velly and Tocqué (Plate 71A) were the ablest imported specimens. Count Shuvalov, President of the newly-founded Academy of Arts, also invited the French Le Lorrain, Jean Moreau, and Louis Lagrenée, to teach there under contract. Enlightened Russian grandees hunted for budding talent on their vast estates, and began to despatch promising serf boys, naïve young Ivans and Fedkas, straight from their wooden huts, to study art in the Petersburg Academy, sitting at the feet of sophisticated masters newly arrived from the Paris of Louis XV.

The richer and more cultured noblemen spared themselves no trouble and expense in training their own serf painters, architects, and musicians. Sometimes they were granted legal freedom as a gift from generous masters. But even when they were not freed they received ample opportunity for creative work. Ostankino, the eighteenth-century palace of the Sheremetyev family, near Moscow, which miraculously survived the ravages of later vandalism, remains a superb example of such fruitful collaboration between art-loving landowners and their own serf craftsmen. Some of these humble nameless artists, who painted excellent portraits, but only of their masters' family, achieved results which would have won them lasting fame, and acquisition by national museums, had they worked in western Europe (Plate 71B). But under less pressure from exacting local masters they might have done far worse, or even made nothing of importance.

Count Bezborodko was one of many grandees who carefully trained his gifted serf carpenters, whom he treated with the utmost kindness, to copy and adapt first-class Louis XV and Louis XVI furniture, which he had brought from Paris. The energetic French Court painter, Madame Vigée Le Brun, who came to work in Petersburg after the French Revolution, recorded with astonished admiration in her memoirs: 'I see here Russians who are ordered to be sailors, huntsmen, musicians, engineers, painters or actors, and who become all these things according to their master's will. And they are all alert, attentive, obedient, and respectful.' She paid high tribute to the moral discipline and touching personal loyalty shown by many serfs, and noted that she never saw a drunken man in Russia and never heard of thefts. She explained that the Russian common people owed a lot of their surprising virtues to that severe discipline which serfdom imposed on them, and how many believed that, if their bonds were removed, they would be no happier.

L. Tocqué, though a pupil of Nattier, a contemporary and compatriot of Fragonard and Boucher, does not appear to have reproduced on Russian soil their familiar strain of graceful, carefree and polished sensuality. An excellent draughtsman, he painted with an eye for underlying character, as well as for polished perfection of technique (Plate 71A). He flattered his sitters less than the average Court painter. Elisabeth was displeased with his too-faithful rendering of her short snub nose, and commanded that it should be lengthened for all subsequent engravings. We know that Rokotov enthusiastically admired Tocqué's portraits and copied many of them.

Perhaps the most influential contributor to the formal style of Russian portrait painting was the Austrian, J. B. Lampi (the Elder) (1751–1830), who became Court painter to Catherine II, and took responsibility both for launching the brilliant V. Borovikovsky and for helping D. Levitsky. A master of the art of knowing how to make people look like what they aspired to be, he could endow his distinguished sitters with a gracious smile, a firm and masterly serenity, or a captivating grandeur. Both he, his near contemporary, the Swede A. Roslin (1710–93), and his protégé, Borovikovsky, were adepts in rendering discreet jewellery, imposing backgrounds, exquisite lace frills, and the fluid folds of gorgeous silk and velvet draperies (Plates

72A and B). The complex human truth is partly hidden under noble masks, not because the courtly artist is unaware of it, but because it might be too ugly, harsh, and painful.

Even as many portraits of our day, obsessed with unmasking naked factual reality, revel in dreary deformity and squalor, so did the portraits of Lampi, Borovikovsky, and Levitsky, select and dwell lovingly on the most attractive and splendid aspects of Russian life in Catherine's reign. They deliberately avoided coarse and nasty details which might offend a fastidious beholder's imagination. Lampi's picture of the capricious semi-Asiatic Potemkin makes him look more like a victorious Roman Emperor (Plate 72A). He interpreted the astute German autocrat, Catherine II, as a stately but benevolent Juno. But Lampi never forgot the debt he owed to Catherine's patronage. One day in the Vienna of 1850 a ragged and nearly blind man, led by a poor young girl, called to see Prince Gorchakov, the Russian Ambassador to Austria. 'Prince,' he said, 'I am the grandson of the painter, Lampi. My grandfather expressed the wish that the sketch of the first portrait he made of Catherine the Great should always be preserved by us. But destitution now forces us to part with it, and I beg Your Excellency to come to see it.' The Prince went to the house. Not without emotion, he saw a small lamp burning below the painting, as in front of sacred images in Russia. This fulfilled a deathbed wish expressed by Lampi, who wanted thus visibly to perpetuate his gratitude to the patroness to whom he owed so much of his success. Prince Gorchakov bought the painting. The Swedish Court painter, A. Roslin (1710–93), painted Catherine in a grand manner, similar to that of Lampi (Plate 72B). Catherine presented one version of his full-length portrait of her to Lord Walpole, when she bought for the Hermitage the latter's famous collection of Old Master paintings at Houghton. It still hangs in one of the spacious galleries at Houghton Hall in Norfolk.

On the whole Catherine preferred Italian artists to other foreigners, and she liked their capacity for transforming everyday routine into an endless fairy-tale masquerade. In 1762 the indefatigable Count Shuvalov invited S. Torelli (1712–84) to teach at the Academy. His work had the gay and graceful fluency of a Tiepolo. The royal personages whom he portrayed are seen as semi-divinities, graciously condescending to adorn this unworthy earth. He painted a charming portrait of the little Tsarevich, later the grim Paul, as a dreamy boy standing in a resplendent suit of armour in front of a stormy sea, attended by a modest negro page.

V. L. Borovikovsky (1757–1825), descended from an old family of minor Cossack gentry, first studied art with his father, who was a life-long professional icon painter. Catherine was enchanted by two grandiose allegorical paintings which he had aptly done to celebrate her triumphal reception in Mirgorod. He settled in the capital in 1790, and is believed to have worked there with Levitsky. It is known that Lampi befriended him, supported his candidature for the Academy in 1795, and in the following year handed over to him his own studio. Borovikovsky allied a delightful softness of paint texture with precise draughtsmanship, and a superb ability to compose human figures in a naturally graceful grouping. He has aptly been called the Russian Gainsborough, and he excelled in that blend of formal dignity with subtly individual character, peculiar to the best eighteenth-century portraits.

His painting of Countess Kushelev and her two children (Plate 73) is a fine example of that refreshingly natural manner. His penetrating but kindly interpretation of his sitters is well displayed in the way he handles these lively, mischievous children, whom Lampi might have painted more like sweet Italian Cupids. His acute sense of rhythm and the gentle fluid gradation of his grouping come out strikingly in his portrait of the two Gagarin sisters (1802) (Plate 74). This increasingly self-confident construction, and departure from rigid conventional poses, plus the gift to reveal, without obvious flattery, the most attractive inward expression of his sitters, are qualities which Borovikovsky shared with Levitsky, and gave to the best portraits of both artists a breathing vitality, charm, and depth of insight, which justify the claim later made by S. Diaghilev to class them as the two greatest Russian painters.

It is significant that, despite his immense fashionable success, Borovikovsky remained loyal to his first love of religious painting, which he continued to practise whenever he could find the time and opportunity. His best-known icons, painted with an easy mastery of Western perspective and chiaroscuro, were done for the Royal Doors of the Priesthood in the Kazan Cathedral, St Petersburg. His portrait of the Metropolitan Michael (Desnitsky) (Plate 75) conveys a rare conviction of deep religious feeling in the priestly hierarchy. Following the fashion of the times, he also executed numerous miniatures. Borovikovsky never married, but in his later years he adopted a nephew, and took five of his pupils to live with him, among them the later famous *genre* painter, Venetsianov.

D. Levitsky (1775–1822), born in Kiev, was the son of a priest, who became a skilled engraver for illustrating Church books at the local Pecherskaya Lavra monastery. Like Borovikovsky, he belonged to Ukrainian stock, and both benefited by the great advantage of being born and bred in a cultured art-loving family and milieu. When Antropov came to Kiev to decorate the Cathedral of St Andrew, he took Levitsky under his protection, and in 1769 he established him on the staff of the Petersburg Academy, where Levitsky taught portrait painting from 1771 till 1788. He is said to have studied also with the French Lagrenée, and with the Venetian professor of perspective at the Academy, J. Valeriani.

After his first success at the 1770 Academy exhibition, Catherine II commissioned him to paint some of her favourite pupils in the Smolny Institute for Daughters of the Nobility. He finished seven portraits of these sparkling young ladies, who evidently inspired him to work with enthusiasm. The two illustrated here (Plates 77, 78), of Levshina and Nelidova dancing the minuet, are masterpieces of free animated composition, combining strong *brio* with fluid grace, and consummate delicacy of detail. His later portraits of the Empress Catherine, though imposing examples of the academic grand style, are far below the level of his best work, and it is unlikely that Catherine ever posed personally for any of them.

His more straightforward portraits, like that of the Swiss soldier of fortune, Ivan Ribeaupierre (Plate 79), are painted with a bold mastery, and with frank but subtle psychological honesty. The portrait of Princess Dashkov shows well the softness and gentle fluidity of Levitsky's brushwork (Plate 76). The sumptuous enigmatic painting of Madame Poltoratsky illustrates his talent in a rich maturity (Plate 80).

In 1782 Catherine created the St Vladimir Order of Knighthood, and Levitsky was commissioned to paint for the hall of that order portraits of holders of the Grand Cross. He had already painted nineteen of them, when Catherine died. But the Emperor Paul, on his accession, refused to have the series continued, simply because his hated mother had commissioned them. Little is known about Levitsky's quiet, industrious, and unpretentious life, except that, despite his acknowledged artistic eminence and prolific work, he always remained a poor man, and probably became blind in his old age. In 1807 his petition to be readmitted to the Council of the Academy was granted, entitling him to receive a modest pension until his death.

Ninety outstanding portraits attributed to Levitsky were shown in the huge

1905 exhibition of Russian painting in the Tauride Palace, organized by the young
S. Diaghilev. But only fifty of them turned up in the 1922 centenary exhibition in
honour of Levitsky, held at the Tretyakov Gallery in Moscow. One must infer that
a number of Levitsky's paintings left the country, unless they were either destroyed
or hidden away during the 1917 revolution and the chaotic civil war which followed. At present their fate remains a mystery, which time may solve. But he is
now recognized in Russia as a great master of portrait painting, though he is still
hardly known in the outside world, where he appears to be represented only by
one portrait in America (illustrated here)[1] and by his portrait of the French encyclo-
paedist, Diderot, in the Public Library at Geneva.

[1] Plate 76.

63. TSAR FYODOR ALEXEIVICH. Egg tempera painting on wooden
panel. Late 17th century.
State Historical Museum, Moscow.

64. PRINCE SCOPIN SHUISKY. Egg tempera painting on wooden panel.
First half of 17th century. *Tretyakov Gallery.*

65. Portraits (oil on canvas)
of Peter the Great and his
consort, later the Empress
Catherine I. Perhaps by
N. Nikitin, early 18th century.

66. ANNA PETROVNA, elder daughter of Peter the Great, and mother of Peter III. By an unknown artist, but probably painted in Russia before her marriage to the Duke of Holstein in 1727.

67. THE TSAREVICH ALEXEI, SON OF PETER THE GREAT. Tannauer, early 18th century.
The Romanov Gallery, Winter Palace, Leningrad.

68. COUNTESS APRAKSIN. A. Antropov, mid-18th century. Former collection of
Count D. Tolstoy, Petersburg.

69. THE EMPEROR PETER III. A. Antropov. Formerly in the Senate, Petersburg (Leningrad).

70. PRINCE GRIGORY ORLOV. S. Rokotov, mid-18th century. Orlov led the Guards officers' plot to get rid of Peter III and place Catherine on the throne. Former collection of Count Orlov-Davidov, Petersburg.

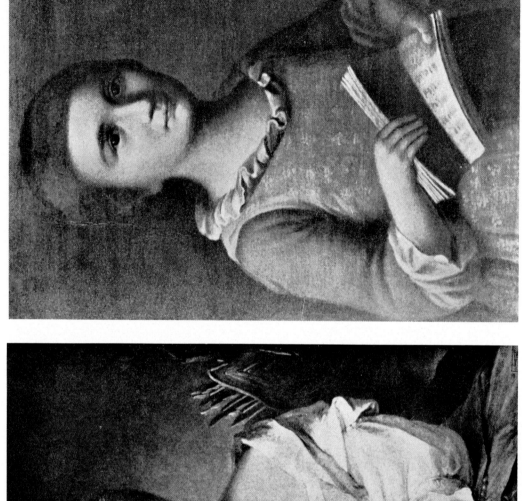

71A. COUNTESS E. R. VORONTSOV. L. Tocqué, mid-18th century. Former collection of Countess E. A. Vorontsov-Dashkov, Petersburg.

71B. AFANASIA NESTEROV. M. Chibanov (serf artist), late 18th century. Former collection of M. Selivanov, Moscow.

72B. CATHERINE THE GREAT. A. Roslin. Late 18th century. *Collection, Mrs May, Washington, D.C.*

72A. PRINCE GRIGORY POTEMKIN. J. B. Lampi (*père*), second half of 18th century.

73. COUNTESS KUSHELEV AND CHILDREN. V. Borovikovsky, 18th century. Former collection of
B. Kotchoubey, Kiev.

74. THE PRINCESSES HELEN AND ALEXANDRA GAGARIN. V. Borovikovsky. Former collection of
Prince A. Kurakin, Petersburg.

75. THE METROPOLITAN MICHAEL DESNITSKY (1761–1818). V. Borovikovsky. Formerly in
Rumyantsev Museum, Moscow.

76. PRINCESS DASHKOV, friend of Catherine the Great, and sometime President of the Academy of Arts. D. Levitsky. Second half of 18th century. *Collection, Mrs May, Washington, D.C.*

77. ALEXANDRA LEVSHIN, dancing the minuet. D. Levitsky. *Grand Palace, Peterhof.*

78. CATHERINE NELIDOV. D. Levitsky. *Grand Palace, Peterhof.*

79. IVAN RIBEAUPIERRE, a Swiss soldier of fortune, who joined the Russian army, and died fighting the Turks in 1790. D. Levitsky. Former collection of Count G. Ribeaupierre, Petersburg.

80. AGATHOCLÉE POLTORATSKY. D. Levitsky. Former collection of N. Romanov, Petersburg.

CHAPTER FOUR

Porcelain of the Russian Empire

Russian porcelain, being little known or collected in the West, has often been mistakenly approached as an inferior or provincial imitation of the more famous German, French, and Austrian factories which preceded it, and therefore deemed hardly worthy of being studied as a ceramic art with a distinct character, artistic quality, and chequered history of its own. But closer acquaintance reveals striking individual features, which not only distinguish it, but enable it to bear comparison with the standard set by the finest western European porcelain, although the first Russian factory started later, and only began to flourish after a series of calamities.

Peter the Great had sent scientific experts on Russian trade caravans to Peking, with strict instructions to find out from the Chinese the carefully guarded secret of the exact manner in which they made their porcelain. But his emissaries returned home disappointed, and none the wiser. It was not until 1744 that his exuberant daughter, the Empress Elisabeth, entrusted a vagrant German, C. K. Hunger, then employed in Stockholm, with a written contract to 'found in St Petersburg a factory for making Dutch plates and pure porcelain, as it is made in Saxony'. Hunger had started life as a goldsmith's apprentice, then sought out Böttger, the famous initiator of hard-paste porcelain at the Meissen factory. He obtained a job there as a craftsman gilder in 1727. He wrote to the Empress Elisabeth boasting that he had been responsible for organizing the Rörstrand ceramic factory in Sweden (whence, in fact, he had been summarily dismissed).

He belonged to that familiar type of brazen adventurers with big artistic pretensions, a class in which even the eighteenth century abounded. Lavish in promises, he knew how to advertise his scanty talents and cunningly win the confidence of highly placed people. In Russia he aroused suspicion when his first firing in the kiln was a total failure, but he continued to find plausible excuses. Finally he exhausted the patience of the director, Baron Cherkassov, who complained that, during three years of so-called *research*, Hunger had turned out barely half a dozen cups, and even these were crooked and discoloured.

XV. (*above*) Dish decorated with exotic birds and border of flowers in high relief. Imperial Factory, Nicolas I, *c.* 1840. (*below*) Dish from dinner-service presented by Alexander I to his sister, the Queen of Würtemberg; centre medallion painted with a view of Carini, Sicily. Imperial Factory, *c.* 1810.

A Russian priest's son, Dmitri Vinogradov, who had studied chemistry in Marburg, was then ordered to extract from Hunger all the secrets of porcelain manufacture, to supervise his work, and never to leave him alone for a single moment. In 1747 he replaced Hunger, who was dismissed. Undoubtedly Vinogradov gave himself heart and soul to practical experimental work, especially with ingredients of the paste and glaze, and scientific methods of firing in the kiln. He produced some outstanding though limited results, but he suffered from bouts of drunkenness, which made him violent and unreliable. Baron Cherkassov took the advance of porcelain seriously, and in 1752 ordered that Vinogradov should be fastened to an iron chain, perpetually watched, and in his turn forced to write down for the benefit of his successors every technical recipe that he knew. He died in 1758 at the early age of thirty-nine. Some exquisitely modelled and painted tea-services and snuff-boxes were made under Vinogradov's direction in Elisabeth's reign, but the quantity was small and specimens are now extremely rare (Plate 81).

After this painful initiation, the Imperial Factory came into its own during the reign of Catherine II (1762–96). She made a thorough personal inspection of the factory in 1763, and at once ordered highly skilled painters, modellers, and craftsmen to be engaged, regardless of expense, from Germany, Austria, and France. Catherine had a passion for building, and for filling whatever she built with beautiful and magnificent objects, without any prejudice about their national origin. For her new Imperial Hermitage and Tsarskoe Selo she collected pictures, sculpture, porcelain, and books from all over Europe. These provided Russian beginners in the arts with truly international standards of the highest class, and a fair chance to overcome their provincial crudity and ignorance.

Reacting against the lush and gaudy baroque encouraged by her predecessor, Catherine promoted a sterner classical temper in architecture, and encouraged a robust architectural dignity in decorative art. Her best and favourite architects were Italians. 'I want Italians,' she told her agent, Grimm, 'because we already have enough Frenchmen who know too much and design ugly buildings.' She bought up all the portfolios of Clérisseau's drawings and aquatints, made during a tour of Italy, minutely depicting Italian ornamental plaster-work, arabesques, monumental vase construction and fanciful Pompeian detail. This lavish Italian strain, often nostalgically reflected by northern temperaments, featured prominently in Russian porcelain, and recurred throughout the following century. At the same time

Catherine herself, being a pure German and a usurper, made keen efforts to remedy these defects by personifying some more ideal aspects of her adopted country, and she tried to give wider scope for native Russian themes in art.

Many western European porcelain factories had begun by working either in the manner initiated by the Chinese or by their immediate European predecessors, and by honestly copying what they most admired. The first Russian factory was no exception, for it emulated Meissen as the acknowledged best and leading exponent of ceramic art. Catherine ordered a well-known dinner-service from Meissen (called *The Hunter's Service*, because it was painted with lively hunting scenes). But, characteristically, as soon as some plates and dishes got broken, she insisted that the Imperial Factory should learn to make all replacements. And these turned out hardly inferior to the originals, although the paste was less uniformly white, showed the bluish tint of Russian kaolin, and the painting was recognizably freer in its brushwork and more naïve in feeling.

The Chinese Empire, being uncomfortably close, appeared less romantic to Russia than it did to western Europe at this time. And the Western fashion for fantastic whimsical *chinoiseries* found less favour there. Moreover, in Russia any craving for the exotic could be amply gratified at home. A book by the German traveller, J. Georgi (translated into Russian in 1776), *Description of the Races inhabiting the Russian Empire*, attracted attention chiefly by its skilful coloured illustrations of striking racial types and their decorative costumes. These formed the starting-point for a long series of porcelain figures, showing picturesque national representatives poised in their regional dress (Plates 82A, 82B).

No doubt they were partly inspired by earlier racial figures made by the famous Meissen modeller, Kaendler, but they drew upon original and local raw material. Their striking success led to the creation of a further series, portraying Russian peasants, tradesmen, craftsmen, etc., wearing their professional clothes and carrying the tools and emblems of their daily work. These provide delightfully idealized *genre* studies of Russian life in the late eighteenth and early nineteenth centuries (Plate 86).

Jean Rachette, son of a French sculptor, but born and trained artistically in Copenhagen, came to the Imperial Factory as a modeller in 1779. He was responsible for launching these two series of porcelain figures, which were outstanding both in their balanced rhythmical composition, their pure, sensitive modelling, and their colourful originality. This foreigner's talented interpretation of native

81. (*centre*) Cup with cover and saucer, decorated with stylized banners and the monogram of Grigory Orlov. The cover is surmounted by two strikingly modelled embracing children. Bears earliest mark of Imperial Factory, used only during reign of Empress Elisabeth. Orlov's initials were added under Catherine II. *Collection, Mrs May, Washington, D.C.*

Russian themes opened a new range of creative opportunities, drawn and enlarged upon by later Russian porcelain factories throughout the nineteenth century (Plate 87). Rachette remained active until 1804, when he was granted the rank of State Counsellor in recognition of his great services to art. Paradoxical though it sounds, foreign artists who came to work in Russia were often more creatively inspired by Russian scenes and subjects than were native artists, who went out of their way to imitate the latest Western fashions, regardless of their quality.

Another feature, developed in the Imperial Factory at this time, glorified Catherine and the achievements of her reign. On many vases her head appears in medallion form wearing the helmet of Minerva. On one a Cupid crowns with a laurel wreath her interlaced initials, while a double-headed eagle holds out an olive-branch of peace. A vase at Gatchina depicts her greeted by a whole group of allegorical female figures, *Abundance, Humanity, Science, Justice,* and *Industry,* while *Chastity,* with modest downcast eyes, held up a mirror to the Empress. The so-called *Arabesque Service,* though decoratively inspired by frescoes excavated at Herculaneum, also served to illustrate recent Russian naval victories over Turkey.

But the majestic dinner-services and vases, ordered by Catherine, already differed both in colouring and form from Meissen porcelain of that period. They were severer, more compact in line, less elaborate and mannered in execution (Plate 83B). In the *Cabinet Service* (first ordered as a present for her favourite, Count Bezborodko) the splendour of luxuriant Italianate ornament prevailed over national self-glorification. Together with exquisite detail, similar to that in the Arabesque Service, it is distinguished by a broad gold band, encircled by garlands of delicate flowers, with oval medallions in the centres, depicting Italian architectural scenes, sometimes with human figures.

Having mastered ceramic technique in the eighteenth century, the art of modelling, painting, and gilding porcelain reached its high point and boldest native originality in the first half of the next century under Alexander I and Nicolas I (Plate XV). But preoccupation with new experiments in rich colour contrast led to a diminishing concern for purity of sculptural composition. This resulted in a looser relationship between formal design and painted decoration. The latter tended to predominate. Intense malachite and emerald greens, rich *lapis lazuli* blue, delicate mauves and buffs and deep maroon, took the place of pure and dazzling white as favourite colours for the background. At the same time, subtle

XVI. (*above*) Part of a tea-service. Kornilov, Petersburg, mid-19th century. (*below*) Part of a tea and coffee service. Safronov, *c.* 1830. This small factory, which lasted only ten years, was noted for its brilliant and original coloured glazes.

miniature painting of flowers, birds or human figures, framed in white panels, was made to blend effectively with these coloured grounds (Plates 90A and B, Plate XVII).

Catherine's son, the Emperor Paul, who reigned from 1796 to 1801, although he was a certifiable megalo-maniac, and hated his domineering mother, inherited her passion for good porcelain. He had a special liking for paintings of lyrical landscapes and fine buildings, and he started a separate branch of the Imperial Factory near his own palace at Gatchina. It is recorded that the day before he was murdered he received a new dinner-service which he had ordered, painted with numerous Russian architectural scenes, and, admiring it together with members of his family, pronounced that day to be the happiest in his whole life.

Alexander I (reigned 1801 to 1825), despite the Napoleonic Wars which dislocated his reign, did not neglect the factory, which continued to recruit first-class artist-craftsmen, regardless of their national origin. As a rule each new foreign craftsman was—sensibly enough—put under contract to teach two Russian apprentices. The most important foreign painter of this period, Schwebach, had worked for twelve years at Sèvres, came to Petersburg in 1815, and was prominent in launching a new *genre* of romantic decoration, depicting soldiers in battle scenes, and Asiatic figures seen against Russian landscapes.

In 1806 Alexander was persuaded to issue a decree imposing a prohibitive tariff on the import of foreign porcelain into Russia. By stimulating internal competition, this measure made private porcelain factories start to multiply. Some were straightforward business ventures, run by enterprising merchants. Others, like that started by Prince Yusupov at his palace of Arkhangelskoe, worked to gratify the taste of wealthy connoisseurs and to provide uniquely beautiful presents for their personal friends. The Miklashevsky factory, started by a cultured landowner who had found china-clay on his estate, and employing his own serfs, won a gold medal at a Petersburg exhibition in 1849. Its most exceptional work was a huge porcelain iconostasis with blue and gold columns, made for the owner's village church at Volokhitin. One generous landowner, who detected an inborn talent for modelling and carving in a young serf called Kudinov, arranged for him all facilities to start his own porcelain factory in 1818, and later gave him his freedom. This factory was, in fact, managed by the Kudinov family, whose name it bore, till 1881, lasting longer than many others founded in the same period, whose economies could not survive the Emancipation of 1861.

The main points of difference between early nineteenth-century Russian and western European porcelain depended less on style (which was then neo-classical throughout Europe) than on choice of themes and mode of artistic interpretation. While the Sèvres factory concentrated on glorifying Napoleon and his deeds, the Imperial Factory started to specialize in majestic and graceful vases with an astonishing variety of shapes and painted decorations (Plates 88, 89). Events of the patriotic war against Napoleon in 1812 also provoked a vogue for romantic-looking battle scenes with soldiers and officers wearing splendid uniforms.

In 1814 the Russians had learned from a French prisoner of war the process of making transfer prints of colour blocks on porcelain. This practice was soon afterwards adopted in Russia by private commercial undertakings. But the directors of the Imperial Factory rejected it as a semi-mechanical device, good enough for the quick salesmanship required by Western bourgeois mass-production, but unworthy of the Russian court and aristocracy, which demanded and appreciated only the finest hand painting.

Nicolas I was more exacting than his predecessor in supervising the Imperial Factory. He required splendid and dignified porcelain to adorn the royal palaces, and for presentation to individuals who had deserved his favour (Plate 92). He examined all important pieces personally, and gave little encouragement to his director's prudent scheme to make the Imperial Factory pay its way by selling surplus products to the general public. During his reign many majestic vases were finely modelled and superbly painted, although some began to show too many scenes directly copied from Old Master pictures in the Hermitage collection. But the most lively and delicate original designs depicted flowers, fruit, animals or exotic birds, and were made on the flat centres or borders of plates, saucers and dishes (Plates 83A, and 92). A leading Russian porcelain painter, Paul Ivanov, excelled in modelling porcelain flowers and foliage in high relief, a technique derived, of course, from the Meissen factory (Plate XV).

The romantic military yearnings of Nicolas I left an enduring legacy in some superb dinner services which he ordered, depicting officers and soldiers of his favourite regiments in their elaborate uniforms. As miniature paintings of the finest detail, these military scenes have a unique quality, and the richly gilded borders of the plates with double-headed eagles on gold or green grounds are more magnificent than anything similar made by Sèvres. The faces and figures of the men, remotely handsome, almost puppet-like, merge in a gorgeous military ballet,

XVII. (*above*) Chocolate cup, painted with scene of a woman carrying coloured laundry, against an Italianate background. Kozlov Factory, *c*. 1840. (*below*) Large cup painted with human groups and view of Palace on the Stone Island, seen across the water. Imperial Factory, *c*. 1820.

where fantastic shakos, perfectly fitting coloured tunics, flying banners, and prancing mettlesome horses dominate and submerge the human element (Plate XVIII). At the 1851 International Exhibition in London, at the Crystal Palace, the Imperial Factory was awarded a medal for its exhibit.

During the reign of Alexander II (1855–81) porcelain orders for the palaces and members of the Imperial family rapidly declined (Plate 93). Emancipation of the serfs in 1861 also led to the closing down of numerous private factories, which had depended on expert serf craftsmen, trained by their enterprising masters and by foreign artists imported for that purpose. Wealth was passing from the often unbusinesslike aristocracy to the more astute merchant class. Taste grew somewhat stereotyped and stale, and art began to be overshadowed in importance for its potential patrons by the growing concern with social and economic reforms.

In 1871 the Empress told the director of the Imperial Factory that he must fight against academic stagnation, by aiming at more vitality, diversity of shapes, painting, and design (Plate 96). She suggested that he might start to learn some useful lessons from English porcelain. The chief sculptor, Spiess, was thereupon despatched to England, whence he brought back numerous specimens from English factories. Despite the decline of initiative among its patrons, the Imperial Factory still employed superb artists, and the flower painting on some of its nobly proportioned vases remained as perfect as before, reminiscent of the most luxuriant Dutch seventeenth-century still-life *genre* (Plate XXI).

Alexander III (reign 1881–94), soon after his accession, gave orders for the Imperial Factory to be granted the best possible technical and artistic opportunities. A survey taken at this time disclosed that a grossly disproportionate number of administrative officials demoralized the most gifted craftsmen, and that many incompetent workmen were engaged or retained, merely because they happened to be children or relatives of members of the staff.

Regularly once a year Alexander gave instructions to the director about projects submitted to him. Far from being a stuffy or indifferent philistine, his own taste encouraged a dignified and massive simplicity (Plate 91A). Towards the end of his reign, however, he showed a preference for the pale cold blues and greys of the late Copenhagen style. He ordered one important and elaborately painted dinner-service for the Court. This was called the *Raphael Service*, because the motifs in it were taken from Raphael's Vatican Loggia, which Catherine the Great had copied in the eighteenth century for the Hermitage in Petersburg (Plate XXII).

Incidentally, the copies, quite good ones, are now better preserved than the originals in Rome.

Under Nicolas II (1894–1917), who had poor personal taste and no love for art, the standard rapidly declined. During his reign little original work was done, except in Easter eggs (Plate XXIII), and the finest porcelain consisted of well-executed additions or replacements to services previously commissioned by his more cultured predecessors.

The first mark of the Imperial Factory in the reigns of Elisabeth and Peter III consisted of a black, impressed or gilded double-headed eagle, and more rarely an

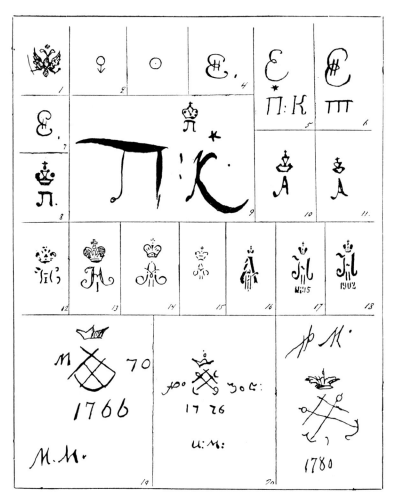

XVIII. Plates with richly gilded borders, and centres painted with officers and soldiers of Russian regiments. From dinner services ordered by Nicolas I. Imperial Factory, *c.* 1830.

impressed anchor. From the time of Catherine II, and under all subsequent emperors, the mark consisted of the reigning sovereign's initials painted under the glaze, usually in blue, but sometimes in black or green. Except in the reign of Catherine, these initials are surmounted by the Imperial crown. Some pieces, made in the reign of Alexander II, have the Emperor's initial, surrounded by a circular wreath. Many earlier pieces are unmarked, since marking was first made compulsory by Nicolas I, and even his stern decrees were not invariably obeyed.

Though the Imperial Factory, to start with, launched the style and themes for other Russian porcelain manufacture, it was followed and frequently surpassed in quality by several private factories, founded in the eighteenth and early nineteenth centuries. The most notable of these was started about 1756 by an English man of business, Francis Gardner, who appears to have first settled in Russia in 1746. The enterprise was successfully carried on by his family and descendants until 1891, when it was sold to the giant Kuznetsov porcelain and faience combine. The factory started in the Gjelsk region, where local white clay, which proved suitable for porcelain, had been discovered. Gardner began by engaging a German manager called Gattenberg, who later went over to the Imperial Factory, and he employed a leading German painter, Kestner, But these and other foreign experts taught many Russian craftsmen, principally serfs, who gradually replaced their masters, as soon as they had acquired the various techniques. Thus the number of foreigners employed in key positions steadily diminished in course of time.

Eighteenth-century Gardner groups and figures of a sentimental pastoral character stick closely to Meissen prototypes, and so do its rare figures representing characters from the Italian *Commedia dell' arte*. The unassuming academician, G. Miller, who visited the Gardner Factory in 1779, noted with surprise that 'its quality is equal to that of any foreign factory'. He found only one defect, that 'its glaze is less white than the Saxon. But they are trying to remedy this and have gone quite far towards success'.[1] Not only could Gardner compete in artistic standards with the Imperial Factory, but he even obtained orders from the Court of Catherine the Great for specially designed table-services. Miller remarked with admiration on the beauty of one of these, decorated with architectural scenes and classical ornament. Gardner made for the Court four complete dinner-services, decorated with emblems of the recently instituted Russian orders of knighthood (Plate 84).

---

[1] *Farfor i Fayans Rossiyskoy Imperii*, p. 22, Vladimir, 1903.

By the beginning of the nineteenth century the Gardner artists, while still learning from foreign models, had grown emancipated from copying them. In particular their figures of Russian peasant types and urban craftsmen maintain a modest and dignified simplicity, unaffected by the increasingly mannered sophistication of Sèvres and Meissen figures at that time. The best of them also excel in expressive modelling and balanced sculptural poise, together with a bold and brilliant range of colour combinations, which often skilfully contrast *mat* and glazed painting used on the same figure. All these innovations and refinements reveal how Russian porcelain modellers and painters, freshly inspired by this new art, were growing in self-confidence, and reaching beyond what they had learned from foreign teachers. They developed individual native themes and original modes of colouring drawn from their contemporary Russian environment (Plate XX).

The Gardner factory could not escape the general decline in visual art which clouded the second half of the nineteenth century throughout Europe. But in a number of unique products it still kept up the more exacting standards of an earlier age. Some of its figures of national types, especially Asiatic ones, are modelled with extraordinary finesse and rhythm, though their colouring tended to be cruder than in the previous decades. But many peasant figures of this period are heavily mannered and 'literary'. They can be painfully coarse and clumsy, looking like drunken, dissolute caricatures of their serene and charming predecessors. In this period Gardner also embarked on mass-produced tea-services, gaily painted with red roses in white medallions against deep blue, red or green grounds. Many of them were made for export to the Turkish Empire or Central Asia, and carry Arabic lettering under the Gardner factory mark. They are widespread enough to be familiar to many people who have never set eyes on the finer and rarer kinds of Russian porcelain. In the eighteen-eighties the eccentric Alexei Gardner ordered his factory to make a life-size figure of himself in pure white porcelain. When his mother pronounced it to be hideous, he broke it to pieces with a hammer, had a red carpet laid between his house and the river, walked down it carrying the fragments, and ceremonially threw them into the water.

Gardner porcelain had a wide variety of marks in the hundred and forty years of its existence. Different shapes of the Latin letter G, painted underglaze in blue or black, were most frequent in the late eighteenth and early nineteenth centuries. Occasionally a mark was used similar to the Meissen crossed swords with a star. In the first quarter of the nineteenth century the full name of the factory, impressed

XIX. (*left to right*) Girl in blue trousers leaning on a beer-barrel. Gardner Factory, mid-19th century. Lady in red *sarafan* and blue *kokoshnik*, with a spaniel dog. Kornilov Factory, mid-19th century. Young gentleman with a dog and a young lady in a pink dress. Popov Factory, early 19th century.

XX. (*left*) Sweetmeat dish in the form of a bunch of purple grapes. Popov *c.* 1840.
(*right*) Bread and salt plate, with elaborate floral border and gilded double-headed eagle against a cobalt blue ground. Popov. *c.* 1840.

either in Latin or Cyrillic characters, became more frequent. In the second half of the nineteenth century the mark is usually the Moscow St George and Dragon crest, surrounded by a circle, bearing the full name of the factory, at first impressed, later painted in green or red. In the last decades of the factory's existence the double-headed eagle was added to the design, and this elaborate mark continued after the Gardner firm had been absorbed by Kuznetsov in 1891.

One of the most important factories, stimulated into existence by the protective tariff of 1806, was started in that year in the village of Gorbunov, near Moscow, by a certain Karl Milli. In 1811 it was taken over by a Moscow merchant, A. Popov, who gave his name to the factory, which, together with his son, Dmitri, he personally built up and directed until he died in the 1850s. A decade later it was sold by the Popov family, and then passed rapidly from one new owner to another. In the 1870s it belonged to an Armenian, and finally passed to a Russian merchant who liquidated the enterprise.

The Popov factory made a substantial profit out of cheap and gaudy porcelain services, which it designed for country inns. But it also specialized in a small output of extremely fine artistic pieces (Plate 85, Plate XX). The latter were carefully designed for a very limited clientele, which had both taste and money. The Popov porcelain highly valued by collectors, even in the nineteenth century, consisted of figures, especially of dancing peasants in gay regional costumes, and elaborate dishes featuring flowers or fruit, sometimes in high relief, which in the quality of their modelling and painted decoration equal the best of the Gardner and Imperial factories. There is a remarkable figure of a negro in the Sèvres museum, illustrating Bernadin de St Pierre's novel, *Paul et Virginie*. Magnificent large-scale ceremonial bread and salt dishes with gilded double-headed eagles and brilliant floral garlands round the border, were another speciality of Popov (Plate XX). The mark of this factory during the whole period of its existence consisted of an impressed or underglaze blue monogram, showing the initials of the founder.

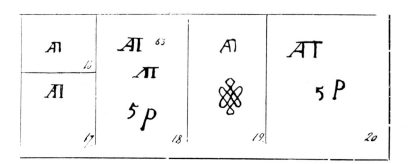

A number of small factories, started during the Napoleonic Wars, were short-lived, and their better products are now extremely rare. For example, the Batenin factory, founded in Petersburg in 1812 by a merchant of that name, lasted only until 1839. Like Popov, it followed the policy of making cheap tea-services for maximum profit and a small output of artistic pieces for the connoisseur (Plate 94).

Some of its vases were outstanding, especially in their original style of floral decoration on mat gold grounds.

The Kornilov factory, started in 1835 by two brothers of a merchant family in Petersburg, engaged highly skilled artists and craftsmen from the Imperial, Gardner, and Popov factories, with which it successfully competed. It quickly acquired a reputation for artistic excellence, and as early as 1839 won a gold medal at the Moscow Ceramic Exhibition. The owners spared no trouble or expense to bring their porcelain to perfection. For this purpose they commissioned many original drawings and designs from leading artists of the day. The gorgeous enamel colours, milky white glaze, rich gilding and decorative *finesse* of Kornilov products soon became well known, and they were sought after by discriminating collectors (Plate XVI). But they remained expensive, compared with similar porcelain from the Gardner factory.

In the last decades of the nineteenth century Kornilov started mass production of cheap porcelain wares for export. Connoisseurs can detect the difference at a glance. The distinction is made still easier by the fact that all the Kornilov porcelain after 1861 is marked with the full name of the firm in underglaze blue, whereas prior to that date similar marks had always been in red.

In 1817 there existed about forty-five porcelain factories in Russia, many of them very small. By the 1870s the number had risen to seventy, but it fell back to fifty towards the end of the century. As industrial organization advanced, the larger factories swallowed up the small ones, or forced them out of business. By the beginning of the twentieth century the giant M. Kuznetsov combine had eliminated so many competitors that it was responsible for about two-thirds of the total annual output of porcelain and pottery throughout the Russian Empire. Though at first it made valiant efforts to maintain characteristic features of the smaller factories which it had absorbed, it was gradually swept along the easier line of cheap mass production.

The Imperial Factory alone, which stood outside commercial competition, escaped from the degeneration of a period in which cheap prettiness and ephemeral popular novelty were rapidly conquering pure artistic merit, as dominant factors in the wider modern market. Working chiefly for the court, the Imperial Factory managed to maintain a surprisingly high level of skilled craftsmanship up to the very end of the nineteenth century, and even during the uninspiring reign of Nicolas II.

After the October Revolution of 1917, the Imperial Factory came to an end, but was soon started up again and re-named the State Factory. The Soviet authorities then called in artists to paint suitably proletarian subjects, jaunty Red Army men and sailors, heroic factory-workers, on an inherited supply of porcelain pieces, previously modelled and baked in the kiln, but not yet decorated or glazed. White unglazed portrait busts of such popular heroes as Karl Marx, Lenin and Maxim Gorky, were also produced in quantities.

In many cases the new Soviet blue hammer and sickle mark was superimposed on pieces already marked with the monograms of the last two Emperors, Alexander III and Nicolas II. Later the products of the State Factory grew more varied and returned to more traditional designs.

For those who can study it with clear standards of comparison, Russian porcelain of the eighteenth and nineteenth centuries appears undoubtedly to form a unique and brilliant artistic phenomenon. Learning with avid zeal from the earlier established European factories, in particular from Meissen, Sèvres, Vienna and Fürstenberg, Russians mastered their techniques, adapted their many shapes and themes, and soon launched out into subtle native variations.

Encouraged, first by a discriminating court and aristocracy, later by an enterprising merchant class, employing craftsmen, whether free or serf, whose patient desire to excel in mastery of an intricate art was not yet dimmed by greed for gain, the leading Russian porcelain factories achieved in their best products a highly individual style, most notably original in its healthy freedom from affectation, combined with bold and vivid colour schemes.

XXI. Monumental vase, painted with flowers and foliage on a deep maroon ground,
with gilded acanthus leaves modelled in low relief round base and centre.
Imperial Factory, *c*. 1860.

82A. (*above*). Kirghiz man and woman, wearing the costume of that part of Central Asia. Gardner, 19th century.

82B. (*below*) Figures of a Mordovinian and a Cheremetian woman in regional costume. Gardner Factory, late 18th or early 19th century. *Collection, Emile Bustani, Beirut, Lebanon.*

83A. (*above*) Plate painted with armorial symbols of Order of St Andrew in yellow medallions on a blue ground. Imperial Factory, *c.* 1830. *Collection, Mrs. May, Washington, D.C.*

83B. (*below*) Champagne cooler, painted with border of roses and a landscape scene in medallion. Imperial Factory, 18th century. *State Museum, Kuskovo, U.S.S.R.*

84. Candelabra in green and white porcelain, combined with gilt bronze mounts and rams' heads. Made for dinner service ordered by Catherine the Great for the Imperial Order of St Vladimir. Bears the motto *For Service and Bravery*. Second half of 18th century. *Collection, Mrs May, Washington, D.C.*

85. Coffee-pot, painted with delicate landscape scene, contrasting with vigorous design of spout and handle. Popov Factory, early 19th century.

86. Three porcelain figures. (*centre*) Lady in blue and gold *sarafan*, carrying two baskets. (*right*) Young cobbler, wearing the costume of his trade. Gardner, *c.* 1830. (*left*) Wandering pilgrim. Gardner, *c.* 1825.

87. (*left*) Boy carrying a potted plant. Gardner, late 18th century. (*right*) Russian dandy, wearing raspberry-coloured coat, salmon-pink waistcoat, and gold-spangled sky-blue breeches. Kornilov Factory, *c.* 1840. *Private Collection, London.*

88. Vase, with Empire style handles, painted with flowers, fruit, and a bird pecking at cherries. Imperial Factory, *c.* 1820. *Collection, Mrs May, Washington, D.C.*

89. Monumental vase in green and gold, with gilded bronze rims. Imperial Factory, *c.* 1830.

90A. (*above, left*) Plate painted with iron-red monochrome portrait of Anna Petrovna, elder daughter of Peter the Great. Imperial Factory, second half of 18th century. (*right*) Plate painted with multi-coloured flowers, butterflies and exotic bird. Imperial Factory, *c.* 1830.

90B. (*below, left*) Plate depicting woman carrying a bundle, with Italianate background. Gardner, *c.* 1800. (*right*) Plate with open coloured rim, depicting a Yakut woman in national dress. Imperial Factory, *c.* 1810.

XXII. (*above*) Plate from Raphael Service, ordered by Alexander III. Imperial Factory, *c.* 1885. (*below*) Plate painted with fruit and flowers against white and raspberry-coloured ground. Imperial Factory, *c.* 1840.

91A. (*above, left*) Teapot in purple and gold, painted with bouquets of flowers in oval medallions.
Imperial Factory, mid-19th century. (*right*) Coffee-pot, bearing cypher of Alexander III in purple and
gold against pure white ground. Imperial Factory, late 19th century.

91B. (*below, left*) Hot-water jug, showing Turkish influence on design, painted with floating flowers and
gilded arabesques. Kornilov, mid-19th century. (*right*) Coffee-pot, Imperial Factory, *c.* 1840.

92. Sauce-boat and dish from dinner-service, painted with animals, fruit and flowers in white medallions. Imperial Factory, c. 1840. *Collection, Mrs May, Washington, D.C.*

93. (*left*) Ceremonial bread and salt plate, with floral border against claret-red ground. Three medallions depict coats of arms of Moscow, Petersburg, and of Alexander II's consort. Mid-19th century. (*right*) Plate with border of gold foliage on emerald green ground, depicting an officer and lady on horseback. Imperial Factory, *c.*1825. *Collection, Mrs May, Washington, D.C.*

94. Teapot, depicting Alexander Column in Palace Square, Petersburg. Batenin, early 19th century. *State Museum, Kuskovo, U.S.S.R.*

95. Vase, painted with Petersburg architectural scene. Imperial Factory, *c.* 1820.
State Museum, Kuskovo.

96. Large porcelain jardinière in 19th century neo-baroque style, with finely modelled figures glazed in bronze against a dark red ground. Imperial Factory, *c.* 1870.

XXIII. Display of porcelain Easter eggs, painted in various designs and colours, two with monogram of the consort of Nicolas II. Late 19th century.

CHAPTER FIVE

Painters of the Early Nineteenth Century

The reign of the thoughtful and generous-minded Alexander I led Russia into the most mature and mellow phase of her civilized artistic life. Coinciding with the Pushkin period in literature, it proved that the lessons taught by eighteenth-century foreign masters had now been assimilated, if not surpassed, by some of their most gifted Russian pupils. In the first quarter of the nineteenth century a vigorously spontaneous literature and visual art arose, at least equal in quality to similar arts in western Europe. And they developed as a fruitful sequel, full of youthful promise, growing organically out of the previous epoch of apprenticeship to the West, in no way a break with it, or a revolt against its guiding principles (Plate 97).

At the same time this aristocratic international culture acquired a more broadly-based national character by drawing closer in sympathy to the traditional peasants, nearer than the refined and luxurious Western Court arts, cherished by the eighteenth-century Empresses, had ever been. The French Revolution, the war against infidel revolutionary France, followed by Napoleon's invasion of Russia, broke the spell which eighteenth-century France had long maintained over the minds of the Russian upper class. That rude shock, and a healthy disillusion in false idols, helped to forge fresh though fragile links of human solidarity between landowners and their serfs, between brave Russian officers and their loyal men, fighting a common revolutionary enemy and invader.

For the first time haunting peasant songs, ancient dances and regional costumes, native wooden churches with onion-shaped domes, simple peasant huts with richly carved and painted cornices and eaves, became objects of vital concern to the Russian educated class. And the spread of lithography, engraving and book illustration, simultaneously widened the popular range and scope of art, as yet without debasing it. Nor did the search, then starting, for a more truly native idiom, mean that the few major artists of this time were boastful selfconscious Russian patriots, infected by tiresome national arrogance in their imaginative work. On the contrary, Oreste Kiprensky was reputed to be the son of Adam Karlovich Schwalbe, of German origin; Venetsianov, father of Russian genre painting, was descended from Italian ancestors; Karl Bryulov's grandfather came from Germany in 1773. Only V. Tropinin was born a peasant serf, and he appears to have been Ukrainian.

We have scanty factual information about the life of O. Kiprensky (1782–1836). His personal origin is shrouded in mystery, and many of his fine paintings have disappeared in recent times. He is now believed to have been the illegitimate son of an officer called A. Dyakonov, by a serf girl, who married his nominal father, Adam Schwalbe, Dyakonov's butler. His master granted the boy his freedom and sent him, already at the age of six, to learn at the Petersburg Academy, where he studied for nine years, and learned how to handle a pencil with the same delicate precision as a skilled surgeon employs his scalpel. He was also taught to put paint on canvas with such precision that even under a microscope no sign of brushwork could be discerned. His teacher demanded that the surface texture of a perfectly finished painting should be as smooth as polished ivory. But he repeatedly advised him to pay closer attention to human faces and their individual expression, and not to aim at striking effect by pleasing colour schemes and too many inanimate accessories.

Portraiture still held a far lower place on the official 'table of ranks' for art, than edifying themes drawn from biblical or Russian national history. Kiprensky, as a highly promising student, was selected by the Academy to specialize in the historical branch of painting, and in 1805 he won a gold medal for his compactly composed academic exercise, *Dmitry Donskoi*. But his impulsive and impressionable nature was drawn above all to portray the real people among whom he lived. Responsive son of a period of storm and stress, he grew into a visual poet of virile, handsome warriors and gentle refined ladies, a sensitive recorder of high State officials, merchants, authors, actors, and humble folk. Pushkin, Zhukovsky, Count Rostopchin, Admiral Kushelev, the actor Mochalov, a ragged Kalmuck boy, have all survived pictorially on his varied canvases. He created an almost comprehensive portrait gallery of his agitated age, seen in a noble dream of strenuous imaginative endeavour.

The faces of his Russian officers are gravely calm and concentrated, painted with luminous clarity against sombre, suggestive backgrounds, full of mysterious depth. A masterpiece of this genre is his three-quarter length portrait of the resplendent Colonel Y. Davidov (1809) (Plate 100). An easy unaffected poise heightens the impression of inward tension conveyed by this Herculean but elegant figure, standing against a landscape of sharply contrasting light and shade. In his Self-portrait (Plate 99), painted a few months earlier in 1808, he put his own ardent temperament into the disciplined guise of a hard-working artist in an open shirt, with paint-brushes stuck behind his ear. But by 1812 he had already become famous in high society, and unfortunately he believed in the fulsome flattery written by fickle critics. He vainly imagined that the world lay at his feet, tamed by his irresistible artistic genius. Basking in a fame which threw him off his balance, he soon began to long for a true friend, a guardian-angel, who would know how to cure him of his intoxicating thirst for worldly success and easy notoriety.

In 1816 he got another chance to choose between the hard dedicated life of an artist and the gilded meretricious career of a fashionable portrait painter. He left for Italy, where he remained until 1823. Every new country and fresh impression took Kiprensky's soul by storm. Rubens, Rembrandt, and Vandyck (familiar to him through the Hermitage Collection) became each in turn his gods. In Milan he was captivated by Leonardo, and in Rome by Raphael. Later, when he exhibited in Naples his portrait of his father, the local jury of connoisseurs took it for a Rubens, and said he must be deceiving them, until he proved the contrary. There is indeed a timeless quality about Kiprensky's best portraits, which puts him on a level with the great masters whom he constantly admired, without ever becoming their slavish imitator. The French painter, F. Gérard, exclaimed about him with enthusiastic astonishment: 'Cette peinture n'est pas de notre siècle!'

One day in Rome the Italian woman with whom he was living was found burned to death. Kiprensky's young male servant died a few days later in a hospital. Horrible rumours began to circulate about Kiprensky's conduct. Kiprensky claimed that the servant had murdered his female model. He took charge of her orphan daughter, Mariucha, and settled her in a convent school. But a dark shadow of suspicion haunted him and made his life intolerable. He was boycotted in Rome, where boys threw stones at him in the street. The mediocre Russian artist colony in Rome had always bored him, sitting all day long at their easels, and at night meeting at hostelries to drown in litres of cheap wine their fruitless arguments and petty personal squabbles. He never sought their friendship. Only the brilliant Bryulov and the Danish sculptor, Thorwaldsen, filled him with respect. The latter had taken him to the Vatican at night, to see the Greek and Roman statues there lit up by flickering torches, to witness how the cold marble forms could come suddenly to life and warmth.

Tired, irritated, and friendless in the end, Kiprensky returned in 1823 to Petersburg, where he exhibited some new portraits, including one of the young Count D. Sheremetyev, standing at the end of a splendid *enfilade* of reception rooms. Through his friendship with Sheremetyev, he acquired some commissions at the court, painted the frail Empress Elisabeth as Psyche, and, after the death of Alexander I, made a fine sculptural drawing of him in profile, crowned with a laurel wreath. Though his draughtsmanship remained amazingly precise and fluid, his warmly rich scale of colouring began to yield to flatter tones, and his sharp arresting grasp of character gave way to duller genre studies of conventional types, like the uniformed A. Shishkov sitting stiffly in his arm-chair (1825), and the prosaic old Count Kushelev, smoking a *hookah* (1827).

But when he escaped from the forced routine of commissioned portraits, he could still paint masterpieces, inspired by his own chosen subjects. His incisive portrait of the dancer, Telesheva, was painted in 1828 (Plate 101). His *Poor Lisa*, holding a flower in her hand, also completed about this time, is even more perfect in restrained movement and gentle charm of expression (Plate 102).

Like Bryulov, Kiprensky in grey Petersburg seems to have pined for the brilliant light, strong sun, and scents of Italy. The orphan girl for whom he had provided was growing up in Rome. In 1827 he returned there, became a Catholic convert, and married the young Mariucha. But he also sacrificed his integrity, and compromised his art. He now readily accepted to paint to order portraits of people in whose presence he yawned with boredom. He kept on painting the smoking volcano, Vesuvius, because pictures of it were in vogue, copied Italian Old Masters by the dozen, in order to sell them to ready buyers in Petersburg. Strenuous and concentrated work tired him too much, but he wanted more and more money. He even borrowed from his friend, Count Sheremetyev, and wrote with conceited petulance to Count Benckendorf, to say that he ought by now to have been awarded some Imperial decoration in return for his great services to art.

Another sad example of brilliant talent, starting well, but later broken under the wheel of fashionable notoriety and routine, finally surrendering to drab banality, from the painful consciousness of which he struggled to escape by taking to drink and casual love affairs. His work became soulless and eclectic. He wandered restlessly from place to place with his young wife, hoping to find in abrupt change of scene that spiritual stimulus which had burned out within himself. They travelled from Naples to Florence, thence to Bologna, then back again to Rome, where he died in 1836, from inflammation of the lungs.

V. Tropinin (1776–1857), another first-class portrait painter, with a more intimately gentle and homely emphasis than his contemporary, Kiprensky, was born a serf, and sent by his master, Count Morkov, to study under the Russian painter, Shchukin, at the Petersburg Academy. His master granted him his freedom in 1823, and in 1824 he was appointed an Academician. For several years previously he had worked as family painter and part-time servant on Count Morkov's estate in the Ukraine. His portrait of his son (1818) (Plate 106) is a masterly achievement, alive with finesse, warmth and charm. Reacting against the eighteenth-century formal portrait, Tropinin always sought to bring out in his subjects some natural grace and character, to avoid at any price grandiose settings and rigid or artificial poses. He made a very effective and intimate portrait of Pushkin, sitting at his table in a dressing-gown.

In the first quarter of the nineteenth century Tropinin went over to a special type of genre painting, in which he depicted some attractive professional person, usually in a half-length portrait, a lace-maker or spinner, surrounded by typical accessories of her skilled work (Plate 98). Later he made some similar studies of urban types. Because Tropinin's work is always modest and profoundly personal, its healthy artistic qualities have not received the attention which they merit, and which more pretentious or *outré* eccentric paintings would certainly have won.

A. Venetsianov (1780–1847), son of a prosperous market-gardener, maintained the harmonious continuity of Europeanized Russian art (he was Borovikovsky's pupil), and made it serve that happy ideal fusion, then taking place, between the civilized Russian upper class and their remotely primitive Slav peasantry. He never travelled abroad. Unlike romantic artists, who sought inspiration either in the past or future, he frankly loved his own age and country, and expressed a touching confidence in the reign of Alexander I, for having proved what profound spiritual benefit people could derive from a wise and restrained Imperial authority. 'It sometimes seems to me', he wrote, 'that I am not in Petersburg, or the Academy, but in Athens at the Parthenon. There must be some kinship between the third century B.C. and our nineteenth century. Purity of taste, elegance and charm, feed my imagination and fill my soul. Poetry, prose, painting, architecture, all flourish. Our people are being properly developed, both in the political and moral spheres.'

Venetsianov is best known for his delightful genre paintings of Russian country life, *The Harvesting, The Sleeping Shepherd, The Barn, The Morning of a Lady Landowner* (Plates 103, 104). While he sharply criticized landowners who remained 'drowned in the stagnant mud of feudalism', his work constantly idealized the fruitful harmony between responsible working landowners and sturdy peasants, who fulfilled their mutual obligations. In this respect he proved to be a fertile innovator in subject-matter, and the father of a whole Russian school of idyllic native scenes in a dream-like agricultural utopia.

He also became a talented portrait and landscape painter, combining both faculties in warmly intimate pictures, rendered with a lyrical feeling for soft diffused light, gently illuminating human figures and objects, seen in a domestic interior or open field. His landscapes are bathed in a mellow glow, conveying that sense of endless and eternal space peculiar to the Russian countryside. His peasant figures blend with the fields and buildings where they live and work. Venetsianov became more fully appreciated in the later nineteenth century, when his art was welcomed like a luminous and gentle ray of sunshine, which helped to dispel the heavy advancing fog of sordid, tortured or gloomily tendentious paintings.

In 1807 the young Venetsianov left Moscow for Petersburg, where he entered the Civil Service, but spent his spare time copying Italian and Dutch masters in the Hermitage. He worked a lot in pastel, whose clear soft colour schemes he introduced later into many of his oil paintings. In 1808 he started contributing to a *Journal of Caricatures*, which was stopped by the censorship after a single issue, because it satirized too savagely sybaritic grandees, fat bureaucrats, and foolish Franco-maniacs. But he then took up engraving and lithography, and it is now considered likely that he made engravings of Petersburg street scenes for the journal *Magic Lantern* (1817). Numerous lively figures of street vendors from these engravings were later used as models for the picturesque statuettes, produced by the Imperial and Gardner porcelain factories.

He lived for a time with the helpful and friendly portrait painter, Borovikovsky, and worked in the latter's studio. In 1810 his own *Self-Portrait* gained him acceptance as a 'candidate' for the Academy. In 1812 he was appointed an Academician, but despite his efforts he was not allowed to teach there. In 1815 he acquired a small estate in the Tver district, where he lived permanently after his retirement from the civil service in 1818. Healthy reaction against dull Petersburg routine caused many young Civil Servants to retire, and seek a peaceful but more

XXIV. PRINCESS BARATINSKY, *née* Abamelek-Lazarev. Watercolour. A. Bryulov, early 19th century.

useful haven in village life, where they often became enlightened farmers, and discriminating benefactors to their own peasants, for whom they founded schools, workshops, and hospitals. Many found time for further special studies. In 1818 Venetsianov was contributing to that purposeful new interpretation of national history, dear to the hearts of the intelligent Decembrist rebels, for he projected a whole new series of lithographed portraits, to be entitled *Great Men of Russia*, accompanied by a description of their lives.

A painting by the French artist, Granet, *Interior of the Church of the Capuchine Monastery in Rome*, exhibited at the Hermitage in 1820, provoked a revolutionary change in Venetsianov's mode of painting. He was fascinated by its convincing contrast of pure light and shade, and by the skilfully natural grouping of human figures in an architectural interior. Previously he had made studies of his Russian peasants in isolation, though treated always as individual characters rather than as ethnographical types (Plate 105B). Now he said that he had to throw away and forget all the mannerisms he had picked up from twelve years of copying Old Masters in the Hermitage. After a few preliminaries, he started to paint his *Barn* (into which the strong daylight falls sharply through open doors.) In 1824, when his *Barn* was exhibited, he wrote that it was 'very well received, *except* by fellow artists'. It embodied his first successful attempt to paint with both accuracy and poetic feeling a group of peasants engaged in their daily work. He even managed to convey the vibration of a warm summer air linking the landscape with the interior. His *Sleeping Shepherd* (Plate 104), also painted in the 1820s (now in the Russian Museum, Leningrad), achieves the same happy blend of portraiture and harmonious physical environment. It depicts a shepherd boy dozing under the shade of a tree, with a hillock in the foreground, whence stretches a broad and gentle vista of the Russian countryside. His *Harvesting* is another beautifully composed group picture of peasant women, working or resting in a field of corn (Plate 103).

Venetsianov's new method involved determined revolt against the stubborn type of teaching then practised at the Academy. He still believed that only from the Old Masters could a modern artist learn disciplined command of drawing and perspective, that basic 'grammar of painting', which should immediately be applied to live native subjects. A human figure, he wrote, 'should emerge in a painting as natural as the floor on which he stands, or the chair on which he sits'. But the Academy taught drawing chiefly from engravings and anatomical plates, then from Greco-Roman plaster casts, and only in the last resort from nature. He deplored the exaggerated emphasis still laid by the Academy on painting in the historical 'grand style'. But he recommended unflagging study and acute observation in order to master that hard scientific discipline which alone could raise a clever artist from fumbling mediocrity to first-class rank.

After Nicolas I had bought his *Barn* for the Hermitage for 5,000 roubles, Venetsianov wrote that this stroke of good fortune would enable him to dedicate himself to teaching his method and conception of painting to poor but deserving young people. He devotedly gathered together a fair number of eager students, and readily bought good brushes and paint for those too poor to pay for their own. About seventy pupils passed through his school in twenty years. Some were tradesmens' sons, others peasant serf boys, who later made their mark as artists. One of the latter, G. Soroka, turned into a truly brilliant landscape and portrait painter (Plate 107). Unfortunately, after Venetsianov's death, deprived of his kind patron's constant moral support and sympathy, he began to feel hopelessly frustrated, and took to drink.

Another talented serf, G. Mikhailov, came to him in 1834, and borrowed money from Venetsianov to buy his freedom. But he turned out to be treacherous and ungrateful, though later a professional success. For soon after Bryulov returned to Petersburg in 1836, Mikhailov deserted Venetsianov, in order to gain fashionable credit as a pupil of the more famous artist. His finest painting, *Girl placing a candle in the Church* (1842) (Plate 108), now in the Tretyakov Gallery, has an innocent, devout serenity, and an unmistakably native Russian quality, which he may well have learned from his first master, Venetsianov. The careerist Mikhailov later became an Academician, and in 1861 was appointed professor of historical painting in Petersburg.

Venetsianov honestly admitted that about half of his seventy pupils came to nothing. Some had limited innate capacities; others were lazy or devoid of talent; a few shamelessly exploited his rather indiscriminate generosity. A number, instead of continuing his school of painting, were easily seduced by the louder more dramatic style, encouraged by the academic *epigoni* of Bryulov. In later life, while so preoccupied with teaching, Venetsianov neglected his own work, which became monotonous and dim in colouring. In 1838 he entered a picture for a competition, financed by the wealthy art patron, Demidov, on the theme, *Peter the Great at Saardam*. But no award was made. Since his renewed offer of services to teach at the Academy was likewise refused, he continued to teach and work on his own in the country. He was thrown from his sleigh in the winter of 1847, and died at the ripe age of sixty-eight.

K. Bryulov (1799–1852) was undoubtedly the most powerful, vital and versatile Russian artist of his day. His contemporaries, including Pushkin, testified to the magnetic stimulus with which even his speech and personal presence infected them. He was renowned for his striking resemblance to the Apollo Belvedere, with his clear-cut oval face, crisp curls and strong athletic neck. His early self-portraits show this classical Greek physique, but permeated by an energetic will and inward emotional tension (Plate 109). His grandfather came from Germany in 1773 to work as a modeller in the Imperial Porcelain Factory. His father, a wood-carver at the Academy, brought him up so strictly that he was forbidden to eat breakfast until he had first correctly drawn on paper a required number of human figures and horses.

The magnificent collection of European Old Masters at the Hermitage guided Bryulov's first steps in art. He worshipped Velasquez, Rubens, and Vandyck, and copied seven times the Velasquez picture of a monk reading a book. Though he became the Academy's star pupil, he quarrelled with its President, Olenin, and in 1822 he left for Italy at the expense of the Society for the Encouragement of Art, accompanied by his brother, an excellent water-colourist, and later the famous architect, Alexander Bryulov (Plate XXIV). While not allowing his first impressions of Italy to overwhelm him, he wrote with healthy modesty: 'One must first digest four hundred years of successful painting in the past, before one can learn to create something worthy of the present exacting age!'

Not only the great artistic inheritance of Italy overawed him; he was charmed by an unexpectedly refreshing vision of robust and harmonious human beings, living in contented poverty in the lap of a luxuriant nature. His picture *Girl Picking Grapes (Italian Noon)* is a fitting tribute from the sensitive nostalgic Northerner, fascinated by the warmly glowing South (Plate 112). German artists in Rome told him that the perfect finish to a painting, like bloom on a ripe plum, brought to a climax by seventeenth-century Dutch masters, had been irretrievably lost by the moderns. Partly to prove that they were wrong, he felt impelled to paint his *Italian Noon.* Later he painted many scenes from life in Rome, and was officially commended for his *Italian Girl washing at a Fountain* (1825). Bryulov often said that he owed his whole development to Rome, as much to its stimulating and attractive human environment as to its eternal art treasures.

But such work failed to satisfy his consuming ambition. For he felt convinced it was his sacred duty to bequeath to posterity some monumental masterpiece of painting. His visit to the recently excavated ruins of Pompeii made a tremendously disturbing impression on his mind, and he started to create his huge composition, *The Last Day of Pompeii* (1833), in which some human groups were suggested by the actual position of skeletons found lying in the excavations, as they had died when struck down by the molten volcanic lava. This picture, now considered by many as a melodramatic period piece, then evoked the highest praise from eminent contemporaries.

One Italian critic pronounced that it combined the majesty of Michelangelo with the grace of Guido Reni. Pushkin wrote a verse warmly extolling it. The novelist, Walter Scott, spent an hour in Bryulov's studio, gazing in silent admiration. Gogol was inspired to write a striking essay, claiming that Bryulov's picture at last restored to modern art that comprehensive monumental character which, since the days of Michelangelo and Raphael, had been broken up into countless fragments and petty minor genres. 'A bright festival came into painting after a long and stagnant lethargy.' 'Bryulov's picture', he wrote, 'can be called a complete universal creation. It answers the longing of our contemporaries, who, feeling their terrible fragmentation, now try to draw phenomena together into big groups, to single out mighty crises, shared and lived through by a mass of people. . . . When I looked at the painting for the third or fourth time, I felt that the perfect sculpture of the ancients had passed over into painting and been imbued with hidden music. Every human figure in it radiates beauty, even tears and terror become beautiful. His colours burn and dazzle the eye. In a lesser artist than Bryulov, they would be unbearable, but he makes them merge.'

The self-critical Bryulov felt dissatisfied with his *Pompeii*, largely because the figures in it did not stand out in relief to the extent that he had aimed at. While the picture remains a distinct and dynamic rendering of a catastrophic historical theme, its agitated human groups and wind-swept composition do not bear the test of time so well as the wonderfully painted and expressive single heads (Plate 111). *Pompeii* was first exhibited in Rome, then in Florence, where it was enthusiastically received, afterwards in Paris, where it found a cooler public, and finally in Petersburg.

It is notable that over half the oil paintings, water-colours and drawings left by Bryulov are portraits (Plates 109, 110). He started, like Kiprensky, in his manner of using deep, dark backgrounds to show up boldly drawn and brightly illuminated faces and hands. He always reserved the purest and most subtle tones for the face. He had already proved himself a master of the big formal portrait in his *Samoilova* (1832–4). But he was constantly searching for new forms in portraiture, and sought to bring out more spontaneous traits of individual character by painting unconstrained people in their everyday surroundings, or moving freely in the open air. His *Portrait of the Shishmarev Sisters* (1839) is one of his most charmingly successful efforts in this style (Plate 113).

Though Bryulov knew the work of the English Thomas Lawrence and of G. Dawe (the Englishman who painted the Russian war heroes of 1812 for the Winter Palace) he was never carried away by the *bravura* or stilted romantic poses of fashionable portrait painters. Nor was he content to go on repeating good results, already obtained, by a display of virtuoso draughtsmanship and dramatically contrasting light and shade. He felt impelled to try out new colour schemes, and he daringly improvised in composition. He never became self-satisfied or ceased to learn from the Old Masters. 'I should like all my work to be bathed in light, as in Paul Veronese,' he wrote after a visit to Venice. His friend, the artist Prince G. Gagarin (Plate 114), aptly observed: 'Bryulov became later like a musician, so saturated with simple and genuine beauties of harmony that he strove to achieve new effects of dissonance'. In Turkey he started to read Karamzin's *History of Russia* and reflected on the possibility of starting a more 'national' school of Russian painting.

In 1835 Bryulov travelled to Greece and Asia Minor. But while in Constantinople he received an Imperial order to return to Russia, in order to undertake professional duties for the Academy of Arts. While in Petersburg he complained to Pushkin about the harsh climate, which made him ill, and the bullying officials, who interfered with his independent work. Nicolas I suggested that he ought to paint Ivan the Terrible and his wife kneeling before an icon in a peasant hut, showing through the window a view of the Russian capture of Kazan. Bryulov, who had no taste for blatantly patriotic historical painting, heaved a deep sigh, and asked the Emperor whether he might be allowed to paint instead *The Siege of Pskov*. He skilfully evaded painting a portrait of Nicolas himself, for which the Emperor had fixed an appointment, but arrived twenty minutes late. Bryulov had meanwhile walked out, and left a message to say that, since His Majesty was always punctual to the minute, he knew that He must have been detained by more urgent and important business.

Pushkin had written to his wife: 'Bryulov is going to Petersburg with a sinking heart. He fears the climate and loss of independence. I try to console and encourage him, but even my soul goes into my boots when I remember that I am a journalist.' Bryulov's chief work in Petersburg was to paint sacred scenes for the interior of the dome of the new St Isaac's Cathedral. But he caught rheumatism, felt lonely and out of place, and though he retained friendly feelings for the old Academy, he had little use for the new one, rigidly reformed by Nicolas.

In 1849 he returned to Italy, where he stayed until he died. He spent a long time in the villa near Rome of his 'only real friend', Angelino Tittoni, of whom he painted several portraits, some of which have regrettably disappeared. Always an impassioned worker, who took every artistic matter to heart, he never grew blasé. He still spent hours gazing at the frescoes on the ceiling of the Sistine Chapel, and a year before he died he wrote: 'I never loved Michelangelo as much as I do now.' At the age of fifty he remarked that he had lived so intensely that he never expected to survive more than forty years. Having already stolen ten years from eternity, he had no right to complain. But he was still haunted by the craving to create another huge allegorical masterpiece, more perfect than *The Last Day of Pompeii*. In 1851 he made a sketch for a colossal new picture to be called *All-conquering Time*, but it never materialized, and even the sketch has vanished. He died in the following year.

Alexander Ivanov (1805–58), son of Andrey Ivanov, professor of painting at the Academy of Arts, served his apprenticeship in that institution, and in 1826 was awarded a small gold medal for his picture of a scene from Homer's *Iliad*. One of his contemporaries aptly observed about him that here was a genuine artist, with an exacting and ideal sense of mission, who sought uneasily to combine within himself the functions of poet, historian, religious philosopher, and acute observer. It is true that Ivanov deserves to be remembered, rather for what he aimed at, and sincerely struggled to achieve, than for the final outcome and artistic quality of his finished pictures.

In 1830 he went to study in Rome, as a pensioner of the Society for the Encouragement of Art, who told him how grateful he ought to feel to his generous benefactors, and ordered him to report fully every two months to them on all he had seen and done abroad. Soon afterwards Ivanov's father inadvertently displeased

Nicolas I, and lost his post at the Academy. No doubt this shock contributed to the lifelong revulsion which the young Ivanov felt, both against the over-organized art of the Academies, and against the crude career-artists who worked solely to win for themselves financial security and official honours. Yet he struggled in vain to get rid of his own ingrained academic limitations, a certain cautious reserve and stiff formality. His first large picture painted in Rome, *Apollo, Hyacinth and Kiparis* (1830–4), though conventional, has some of the classical quality, vigour, and rich colouring of a mature Poussin. He was finding his feet in Rome, where the sheer number of fresh impressions and abundance of artistic masterpieces tended to overwhelm the new-comer.

Ivanov's diary at this time contains thoughts about the proper relations of the aspiring modern artist to his established classical predecessors. He believed that to admire, however ardently, did not compel to imitate. And he insisted on the need to maintain a receptive humility towards the genius of the past. Visiting Venice (which had been strangely excluded from his official itinerary), he felt enthralled by Veronese, Titian, and Tintoretto; 'from their warm souls they poured on to canvas the full revelation of colour'. The glowing Venetian masters conveyed a special message for an ascetic colour-starved son of the North.

Despite the uplifting environment, Ivanov felt friendless and lonely in Italy, sometimes on the verge of suicide, yet he refused to return to Russia when his scholarship expired. 'The thought of going back to my country makes the palette and brushes fall from my hands and kills my desire to do something worth while,' he wrote in his diary. He persuaded himself that a true artist in this coldly commercial age must learn to live like a hermit, a self-denying holy man, and that his own determined, patient striving would in the end move the heart of the Tsar towards making a happier future for his subjects. He resembled his contemporary Gogol, in his strange mystical belief that an artist could thus help to stir up a radical spiritual upheaval, though, by its very nature, this upheaval would be confined to the few superior human souls capable of experiencing it.

For his sacred painting, *Christ appearing to Mary Magdalene* (1835), Ivanov was elected an Academician. But he wrote disparagingly in reply to his father's congratulations: 'You suppose that a lifelong salary of six to eight thousand roubles, a free corner in the Academy, is a great blessing for an artist, but I think it is a curse. The Academy of Arts is a relic of the previous century. Its present-day mercantile calculations can never move art forward.'

Ivanov had determined to elaborate in visual terms the theme of man's moral renewal in this world, his self-redemption in communion with his fellow creatures. With this arduous ideal in mind, he started in 1837 his vast *The Appearance of the Messiah before the People* (Tretyakov Gallery.) He made hundreds of sketches and variants for this painting, on which, incredible as it may seem, he worked intermittently for twenty years. He filled whole albums with drawings of heads, figures, and parts of the human body. Increasingly isolated and silent with the passing years, he shut himself up in his Roman studio, but persevered in strenuous poverty.

Yet he recognized that his picture, as it advanced, fell far short of the great intentions which he had originally put into it, for he wrote in 1855: 'The big picture sinks more and more in my estimation. We have now gone so far in our thinking that, faced with the latest decisions of learning, the basic thought of my picture somehow gets lost. While leaving the old modes of art, I have not yet built any firm foundation for the new, and find myself, involuntarily, an artist of transition.'

Notable in Ivanov's conception of the expectant people, waiting for their moral leaders, is the absence of any amorphous or faceless multitude. The *crowd* in this painting is wholly formed from a number of distinct characters and individual groups. The prophet, John the Baptist, with a moving gesture, draws the attention of them all to the significant figure of Christ, appearing in the distance. All faces look in his direction, but with an astonishing variety of expressions, ranging from joy, hopefulness, cynicism and anger, to wonder or plain curiosity. In the foreground on the left a simple robust youth climbs eagerly out of the river, to get a good view of the Messiah. Next to him, an old man, leaning on a staff, waits with patient resignation (Plate 115A).

Turgenev pointed out that this picture served as a salutary reminder that we Europeans have entered a period when pure straightforward painting had been weakened and clouded over by an influx of extraneous intellectual problems. 'We must admit it to be a period of decline.' The picture, he said, had glaring defects. The colouring was dry and harsh, there was no air in the foreground, but it stood out, none the less, as 'a great, serious and elevated work'. It would be wrong to call the picture a total failure because it aimed too high or attempted to express in paint the pictorially inexpressible. Turgenev's judgement is sound and penetrating. But even he hardly did justice to Ivanov's artistic success with certain individual heads

184

and figures, which look far better when they can be seen apart from the over-loaded and stilted composition.

Before Ivanov, no Russian artist had painted the human nude, not posing in the art school, but freely moving in the open air. In the *Appearance of the Messiah*, and the many studies which he made for it, Ivanov managed to convey refreshing new impressions of the beauty of the naked human form, seen in a play of light and shade, subtly lit by direct or reflected light from sky, earth or green vegetation. He also achieved hundreds of unexpected colour combinations and characteristic movements, suggested to him by watching Italian boys and girls against the clear, dry Italian summer landscape (Plate 115A). In this respect he foreshadowed certain features in the work of the more genuine French impressionists.

In 1848 Ivanov's father died. A modest inheritance enabled him to stay in Rome till 1857. In the following year he visited Alexander Herzen in London, and then returned to Petersburg. But he had lived a solitary life abroad for twenty-seven years. His parents were dead, his brother absent, his old acquaintances had become indifferent strangers to him. He had to undergo painful and humiliating negotiations to arrange an exhibition of his *Appearance of the Messiah* and the many studies he had made for it. In the end his great picture was received with indefinite reserve, and its acquisition by the Tsar for the Hermitage encountered unforeseen obstacles. Weary, sick at heart, worn out by worry and disappointment, Ivanov died at the early age of fifty-two, after spending only six weeks in Petersburg. A few hours after he died an official arrived from the Court to announce that Nicolas I had bought the picture.

His friend, Herzen, summed up in a deeply sympathetic obituary notice in *The Bell*: 'Unfortunately Ivanov's life was an anachronism. Such reverence for art, such a religious dedication to it, combined with diffidence about his own powers, with fear and faith, we find only in stories of mediaeval hermits, who prayed while they painted, for whom art was a moral struggle and a sacred science.' His latest Soviet biographer, M. Alpatov, has also recorded a significant conversation which Ivanov had in Petersburg with N. Chernyshevsky, then editor of *The Contemporary*. The latter asked him how he conceived the new direction which art ought to take, in so far as that movement could already be made comprehensible to modern people. Ivanov answered: 'To combine the perfect technique of Raphael with the broader ideas of a new civilization. I tell you that art will then regain in the life

185

of society that significance, which it has wholly forfeited today, through failing to fulfil peoples' deeper spiritual needs.'

With all his craving for integrity and independence, Ivanov never tried to be a law unto himself. He felt that, more than ever, in the modern age, an artist must follow some guiding star, to save himself from drowning in the stormy chaos of contemporary industrial barbarism. For him that star remained Raphael, the 'perfect painter', though he recognized how many European artists, even at times his contemporary, Ingres, in their over-meticulous loyalty to classical canons, could degenerate into cold, self-conscious and mannered revivalists. But Ivanov himself, starting from competent academic compositions in the grand style, later managed to excel both in portraiture and landscape painting, and in luminous genre studies, especially of unconstrained nude figures, seen against the clear and glowing Italian landscape (Plate 115B).

We should recall that the tradition of Western painting did not take root in Russia till the eighteenth century. Though Russia produced no Raphael or Rembrandt, her leading artists in oil painting at this time did not fall below the level of their contemporaries who painted in Western Europe. If what Russian painters achieved on canvas often fell short of what they aimed at, they could still leave, like Ivanov, an edifying legacy of endeavour. Even so, they excelled in the sphere of portraiture, and the best work of Kiprensky or Bryulov could bear comparison with that of any European rivals except Goya.

97. V. SUKHANOV. A. Egorov, an artist of Kalmuck Tartar origin. 1812.

98. THE SPINNER. V. Tropinin, *c.* 1820. *Tretyakov Gallery.*

99. SELF-PORTRAIT. O. Kiprensky, *c.* 1808. Former collection of O. Schwartz, Petersburg.

100. Y. DAVIDOV, in the uniform of a colonel of the Hussars. O. Kiprensky. (A cousin of
Denis Davidov, leader of Russian guerilla troops in the Napoleonic campaign of 1812, whose
portrait this was formerly thought to be.) *Russian Museum, Leningrad.*

101. THE DANCER, K. TELESHEVA. O. Kiprensky, 1828. She is portrayed playing the part of Celia in C. Didlot's ballet, *The Hunting Adventure. Tretyakov Gallery.*

102. POOR LISA. O. Kiprensky, 1827. Former collection of Count Sheremetiev, Petersburg.

103. HARVESTING, SUMMER. A. Venetsianov, 1830.

104. SLEEPING SHEPHERD. A. Venetsianov, 1824. *Russian Museum, Leningrad.*

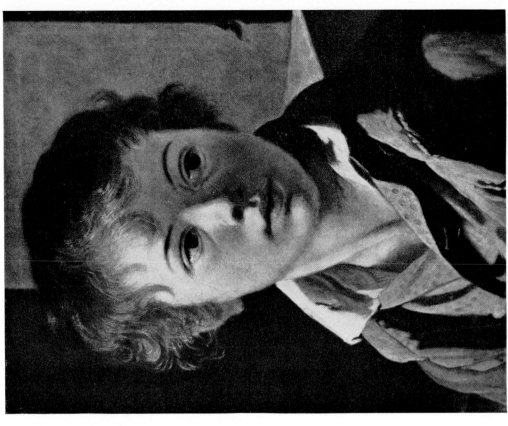

facing page

105A. (*left*) DRAWING OF A PEASANT. P. Barbe, 1824.
Russian Museum, Leningrad.

105B. (*right*) HEAD OF A PEASANT. A. Venetsianov, 1825.

106. PORTRAIT OF THE ARTIST'S SON. V. Tropinin,
c. 1820.

107. PORTRAIT OF E. MILYUKOV. G. Soroka (peasant artist). *c.* 1846. *Russian Museum, Leningrad.*

108. YOUNG GIRL PLACING A CANDLE IN THE CHURCH. G. Mikhailov (pupil of Venetsianov). *c.* 1842. *Tretyakov Gallery.*

109. SELF-PORTRAIT. K. Bryulov, *c.* 1820.

110. Z. HITROVO. Water-colour. K. Bryulov. (A descendant of B. Hitrovo, director of the Tsar's workshops in the reign of Alexei Mikhailovich.) 1832.

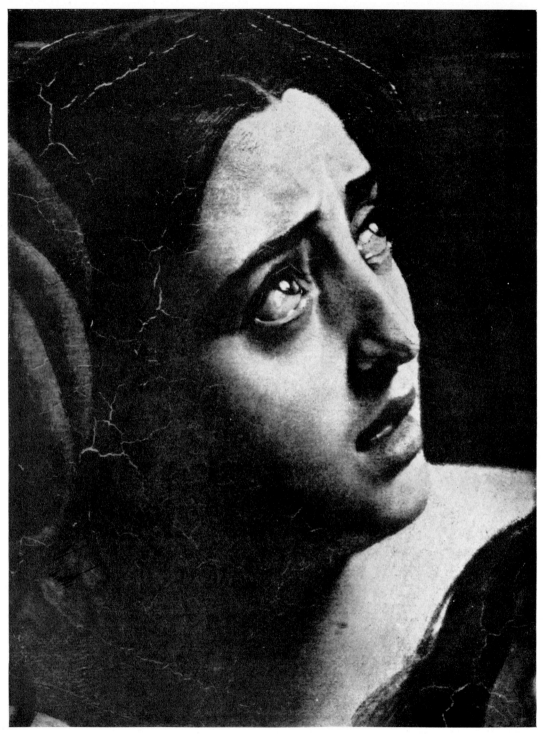

111. THE LAST DAY OF POMPEII (detail). K. Bryulov, 1833. *Russian Museum, Leningrad.*

112. ITALIAN NOON. Italian girl picking grapes. K. Bryulov, 1827. *Russian Museum, Leningrad.*

113. THE SHISHMAREV SISTERS. K. Bryulov, 1839.

114. THE COSSACK FEDYUSHKIN. Prince G. Gagarin, 1840.

115A. (*above*) THE APPEARANCE OF THE MESSIAH BEFORE THE PEOPLE.
Detail, showing a boy and an old man in the left foreground. A. Ivanov.
Tretyakov Gallery.
115B. (*below*) NUDE BOY. A. Ivanov, *c.* 1852.

CHAPTER SIX

Painters of the Later Nineteenth and Early Twentieth Centuries

P. Fedotov (1815–52) son of a poor army officer, started a new chapter in Russian art by first describing, in a pure painter's language, the characteristic street scenes and rising urban bourgeois types of Moscow and St Petersburg. Educated at the Moscow Cadet School, where the birch-rod and the Bible still remained the chief instructors, he survived this strenuous training, entered the army, and soon became admired by his brother officers for his witty caricatures, lively portraits and vivid anecdotal sketches drawn from regimental life. In 1835 he painted a portrait of Nicolas I, in order to pay off a debt he had incurred to a brother officer. After the reception of his ceremonial picture, *Blessing of the Regimental Banners in front of the restored Winter Palace* (1837), he ventured to ask his patron, Grand Duke Michael Petrovich, if he could graciously be granted conditions of life more favourable for the pursuit of painting, the vocation nearest to his heart. The Grand Duke showed this picture to the Tsar, who promptly offered Fedotov release from routine military service, together with a small annual pension.

Before accepting this offer, the modest and diffident Fedotov visited Bryulov, to whom he brought a pile of his water-colours and drawings, and sought the great master's frank advice. Bryulov looked through the works and told him he had still a lot to learn. The writer, Krylov, warned him against the blind alley of settling down as a mere battle painter, since the Emperor would expect him to go on pictorially glorifying military parades for the remainder of his life. So, on second thoughts, he decided to remain in the army till 1844, painting only in such spare time as he could snatch from his arduous official duties.

Fedotov's *Walking in Moscow under the Rain* (1837) showed another new artistic current, a sensitive but precise observation of urban crowd scenes, represented with a gentle touch of humour. And his *Card-Players* (1840) provided a rare example, for that time, of a well-composed and natural group portrait. But

207

Fedotov was rapidly developing, not only into a skilful recorder of current Russian manners but into an acute artistic interpreter of Russian urban life. Much as he admired the 'high art' and intensely noble originality of Bryulov, he had no use for Bryulov's smart academic imitators, with their haughty inhuman heroes surrounded by flying draperies and framed in classical marble columns. He felt attracted by more disturbing contemporary scenes and people, and by subtly instructive urban anecdotes.

After he finally resigned from his regiment in 1844, he noted: 'Only a tenth of my work can be done in the studio, my principal work is in the streets.' For him Petersburg had ceased to be the stately majestic capital of Pushkin's *Bronze Horseman*; he found his themes in the dark damp side-streets and unkempt corners, inhabited by poor artisans and petty down-trodden officials, the long-suffering and pathetic Petersburg underworld of Gogol's *Overcoat*. Here he sketched ragged beggars, wandering minstrels with tame performing monkeys perched on their shoulders, picturesque cab drivers with high hats, and stolid uniformed policemen. He also knew how to poke fun at the habits of pretentious fellow artists (Plates 116A).

But the wealthy merchant class now provided artists both with important new subjects and with indispensable patronage. The small easel-painting, to adorn a cosy sitting-room, designed to suit their more comfortable mode of life, was coming into fashion. It provided a natural reaction against the huge and splendid pictures of the previous generation, created mainly to adorn majestic palaces, churches and country houses. Fedotov's finest paintings became, in fact, illustrative commentaries on Russian middle-class manners, partly social satires, but seen with a sensitive artist's eye and a desire to create, far removed from the coarsely vindictive caricature of his English near-contemporary, Hogarth.

Thanks to Bryulov's persistent help and encouragement, Fedotov's two pictures, *The Discriminating Bride* and *The Morning of an Official*, were exhibited and highly commended at the Academy of 1847. The former picture is painted with the masterly precision of a seventeenth-century Dutch interior. The pathetic inward enthusiasm of the old maid as her hunchbacked suitor, on his knees, hands her a bouquet of flowers, is also admirably rendered. When Fedotov showed him this painting, the generous-minded Bryulov is said to have remarked: 'I congratulate you; you have overtaken me.' For sheer expressive subtlety of character painting in a more complicated scene, *The Major's Courtship* is even better (Plate

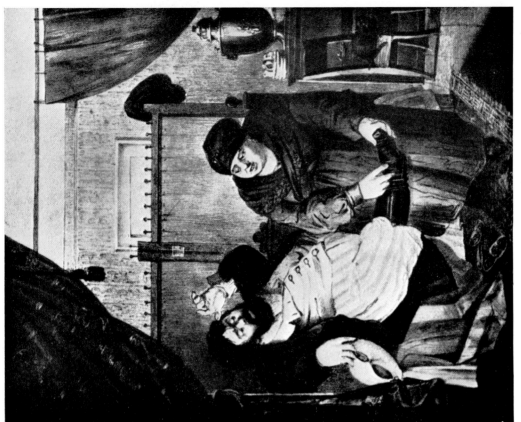

116B. 'Oh, what a hard life we merchants have!' Mid-19th century lithograph by an unknown artist.

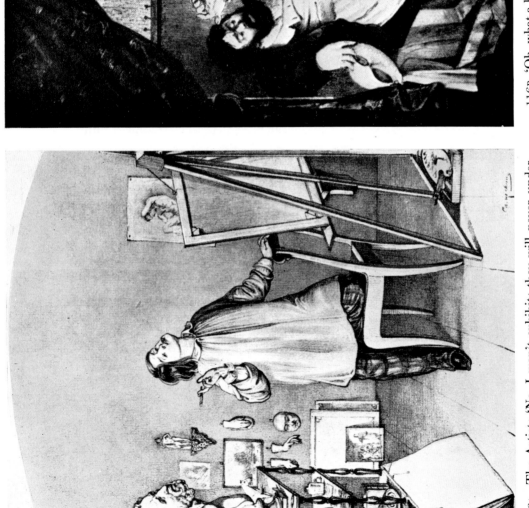

116A. The Artist; 'No, I won't exhibit; they will never understand!' From a drawing by P. Fedotov. Mid-19th century.

117). It received recognition as Fedotov's masterpiece, when it was exhibited at the Academy in 1848, and on the strength of this picture he was elected an Academician.

But this sudden wild success in no way turned Fedotov's head. He noted in his diary that capricious fate still mocked at him. The 1848 rebellions, which shook the feeble thrones of Europe, had induced a morbid fear of honest contemporary art in Russian official circles. Fedotov began to be suspect to the authorities as a dangerous free-thinker, an irreverent social satirist with subversive cravings. The artist had for long been haunted by the fear of sinking into sordid poverty, caused by public indifference to his work. Art patronage in Russia was limited to a small circle, and notoriously fickle. Fedotov had expressed this fear humorously in one of his pictures, called, *The Artist who, relying on his talent, married without a dowry* (1846). In a bare untidy cellar sits a decrepit artist, reduced to painting some commercial shop sign. He has a bandaged jaw and looks like an aged worn-out Fedotov. The cook tears a frame from one of his pictures to stoke the dirty stove. His ugly son brings in a stolen teapot, while his daughter slides through the doorway with a sinister-looking man, who entices her with a necklace.

The whole composition is similar to Hogarth's well-known *Poor Poet*, and there can be no doubt that Fedotov owed a lot to Hogarth, whose work was familiar to him through engravings. The minor Dutch genre painters, whom he had studied thoroughly in the Hermitage, stimulated his polished and mellow refinement of technique. But Hogarth provided him with pungent social themes, and this one reflected a forecast of his own unenviable position. In 1848 Fedotov started a whole series of topical drawings in sepia, intended for subsequent lithography, entitled *Moral and Critical Scenes from Daily Life*.

In vain he tried to steer clear of dangerous or forbidden subjects, which might darken further the cloud of official disapproval now gathering over him. Even as, ten years earlier, he had painted portraits of royal personages in order to pay his debts in kind, so now he painted a graciously benevolent Nicolas I, inspecting a school for young ladies. 'I am accustomed to setbacks,' he noted in his diary, 'through having appeared on the scene as a pure artist in a rowdy political age. I renounced all that is now valued in this world, seeking a new, purely pictorial language.' His painting *The Little Widow* (1850) depicts with gentle pathos the grief of a young woman, leaning against a bureau, on which stands a portrait of her dead husband (a Hussar officer) and an icon of Christ. Despite the total unobjectionability of his latest themes, Fedotov's work was not accepted for exhibition in the Academy of 1851. It seems that after Bryulov's departure for Italy in 1849, the envy and hostility of certain Academicians, hitherto muffled through fear of Bryulov, now vented itself in spiteful pinpricks against Fedotov, and in spreading malicious reports that he had failed to justify official confidence placed in him.

'The newspapers wept, not finding any of my pictures in the Academy,' he wrote in a letter, trying to make light of his disappointment. But patrons, with little independent judgement, began to fight shy of him, and the censors refused to permit publication of lithographs of his earlier genre drawings and paintings. Fedotov began to be haunted by fear and felt forced to be perpetually on his guard. 'I can trust nobody,' he wrote in 1848. He desperately tried his hand in the supremely neutral sphere of landscape. Sometimes Mother Nature could save an artist's sanity by giving him a soothing escape from daily sadness and frustration. But Fedotov could only bring himself to paint the supremely melancholy winter landscape of Petersburg. His last oil painting, *An Officer's Life in the Country* (1852), reflects the inescapable blind alley in which he now found himself to be confined. A young officer, obviously bored to distraction in some stagnant provincial hole, lies outstretched in a dark and miserable hut, engaged in his sole remaining diversion, to make a poodle jump over a stick, and cry: 'Encore, encore!' One day Fedotov went to an undertaker and ordered his own coffin. Later he was found sobbing in the snow by his faithful military servant, who brought him home. Soon afterwards he became violent, was put in a strait-jacket, and he died insane.

During the nineteenth century first Rome, then Paris, became the chief magnetic centres of artistic inspiration for all Europeans, including Russians, who were thus guided by the same Western scale of international aesthetic values, and followed exactly the same sequence of styles and revivals as their Western neighbours. The features of a purely Russian school of painting are not distinctly marked, except by local differences of subject-matter and nuances of individual interpretation. Some Russian artists, after enduring the stultifying rigours of the bureaucratic Imperial Academy, followed the example set by A. Ivanov, and settled permanently abroad. One of the more distinguished expatriates was A. Harlamov (b. 1842), who chose to live in Paris, where he painted well-known portraits of Turgenev, the novelist, and Madame Viardot, the internationally famous singer,

118B. VIEW OF THE WINTER PALACE from the Neva. Lithograph from a painting by Vorobyov. Early 19th century.

and excelled in gently nostalgic studies of gipsies and peasant girls (Plate 124B).

In the later eighteenth century architectural landscape views had almost become a Russian *genre* in the hands of the Russophil Swedish artist, Patterson, who came to Petersburg in 1787. Topographical precision in landscape, animated by groups of human figures, was further encouraged by the School of Venetsianov, and added to the architectural feeling of eighteenth-century engravers (Plates 119, 120). M. Vorobyov's architectural aquatints of Petersburg did justice to the fantastic mystery of the massive Imperial city, seen by moonlight or through a rosy nordic mist (Plate 118B). His better known pupil, I. Ayvazovsky (1817–1900), a tireless romantic, managed to make his style respected in a more pettily prosaic age. In range of gently luminous tone values and mastery of liquid movement, his famous seascapes are unsurpassed (Plate 118A). He tried to merge human moods with untamed elemental forces, seen in the majestic but ever-changing sea and sky.

212

In the later nineteenth century a number of artists, of whom I. Levitan (1861–1900) was the most famous, specialized in painting subjects taken directly from the Russian countryside. *The Ravens have arrived*, by A. Savrasov (Plate 123), combines an unmistakably Russian rendering of lyrical silver birch trees with a typical village background, and an exhilarating sense of the sudden approach of spring. More ambitious painters, like V. Y. Makovsky (1846–1920), preferred to use landscape and provincial scenery as a background for human domestic dramas. Makovsky's *On the Boulevard* (Plate 122) is a striking example of this native Russian episodic *genre*, the raw materials later used to construct so many memorable Chekhov stories.

Perhaps the most unmistakably Russian paintings of the nineteenth century were those devoted to representing scenes of peasant life, seen through the loving eyes of *narodnik* idealists. These are refreshingly superior to heavy topographical studies of the plainly realist school. A. Stryelkovsky's (1819–1904) touching watercolour of a young peasant woman carrying a basket of cabbages, is imbued with all the grace and gentle thoughtfulness of the Slavophil Arcadia (Plate 124A). N. Bogdanov-Byelsky's (1868–1945) well-painted study of a ragged little peasant boy, seated at his rough school desk, reveals (without any sentimental over-emphasis) the uncomplaining dignity of humble rural poverty (Plate 129).

The publication of Chernyshevsky's *Aesthetic Relation of Art to Reality* (1855) marked the beginning of the radical intelligentsia's campaign to grind all self-respecting artists, whether verbal or visual, into tools of social propaganda. Angry topical invective or stirring civic sermons began to be preached as the sole legitimate subject-matter for a *socially useful* art. This obstinate campaign infected painters, as well as writers, with forced self-conscious *tendencies*, which attempted to excuse the most slovenly neglect of craftsmanship in the name of rendering a 'social service'. And it burdened them with a perfunctory leaden weight of banal and prosaic moral messages, which spoiled both beauty of form and spontaneity of feeling.

Though the better artists fought against this degradation of their status, they found it ever harder to maintain high and exacting standards, to which the long-suffering but bored public had grown increasingly indifferent. Hidden under the name of science and humanitarian sentiment, the modern worship of cold analysis and satire, ugliness and shocking deformity, started on its destructive course. The double-headed eagle, with its cruel but disciplined majesty, was yielding to a double-headed dragon, foaming at the mouth with envious rage, conceit and petty spite. The poet Nekrasov's bitter cult of revengeful tears and groans also did a lot to upset that spiritual equilibrium and strong detachment, indispensable for dedication to true creative art.

In this way the discreet and exquisitely elegant social satire of Fedotov was followed by the powerful, still finely executed, but more portentous, genre painting of V. Perov (1833–82). Illegitimate son of an impoverished nobleman, Perov went through the hard apprenticeship of struggling penury. After studying in the Academy, he received a scholarship in 1862, and travelled to Berlin, Dresden, and Paris. But after two years in Europe he asked the Academy's permission to return home before his scholarship expired, explaining that he had already learned enough abroad, and that his work would gain more by a fresh opportunity to paint the uncounted wealth of unexplored subjects, presented by the town and country life of his home land. In 1866 Perov was appointed an Academician, and in 1871 became professor at the Moscow Institute for painting and sculpture. This modest material security enabled him to settle down to work with devoted care on the subjects which appealed to him, without surrendering to the more strident radical demand that he ought to preach plain pictorial sermons.

Certainly topical genre themes from Russian life provided new and inspiring raw material for painters saturated with academic classicism. Both Venetsianov and Fedotov had demonstrated what delightful results could be obtained from watching peasants working or relaxing in their fields, or the normal behaviour of merchant families in their homes. Perov managed to enlarge and deepen the range of human genre studies started by his predecessors. But radical didactic literature tried to enslave painting, by commanding that artists, like writers, should tell an edifying story, 'unmask' the wicked (especially officials and priests), and point some unmistakable moral. Though Perov felt this pressure, he refused to be deflected from his elaborate jewel-like manner of work, skilfully building up a mosaic of finely observed detail, bound together by a genuine and individual emotional integrity, apart from its social content. This firm adherence to the Old Masters' approach to art seemed an old-fashioned defect in the eyes of his crudely simplifying contemporaries, but Perov owed to it his eminence and survival as a major artist.

Though Perov never became a pure colourist, he showed already in his Paris work a subtle sense of tone values and sensitive power of draughtsmanship, despite a sombre scale of colours, verging on the monochrome. He also excelled in combining a relevant landscape with human figures, in order to enhance the emotional mood and intensity of his composition. In his picture *The Village Funeral* (1865) (Plate 125) the tragic resignation of the bereaved peasant and his two children is poignantly blended with the melancholy silent snow scene of the background. Although it might have been made as an illustration to Nekrasov's popular poem *Frost, Red Nose*, the whole picture is too powerfully simple, concentrated, and well painted, to be treated as a mere anecdote of peasant poverty.

His *Tea-Drinking* (1862) (Plate 126) is another finely painted composition on a social theme, though permeated by a sharp anti-clerical satire. A fat contented monk sits comfortably drinking tea (with a bottle of stronger liquor in a bag at his feet), while his servant turns away from the table an emaciated beggar with a wooden leg, who is accompanied by a little boy in rags. The painting of the table-cloth is worthy of Vermeer, and the expression of each human figure is carried to perfection without strain or superfluous detail. Though the boy's face is invisible, his movement of entreaty and pathetic rags speak eloquently enough. The beggar may well have been drawn from some wounded veteran of the Crimean War. Another famous but more blatantly anti-clerical picture by Perov, inferior as a work of art, was his *Easter Procession* (1861), which depicts a number of visibly intoxicated priests staggering out of a village inn.

Perov had also the good fortune to be commissioned by the enlightened Moscow industrialist, P. Tretyakov, to paint several portraits of outstanding contemporary Russians for his new public art gallery in Moscow. In his paintings of Dostoyevsky, the dramatist Ostrovsky, the poet Maykov and the historian, Pogodin, Perov showed himself superior to his contemporary, Kramskoy, in the depth and variety of psychological likeness which he was able to achieve. The prosaic and standardized dress of the mid-nineteenth century professional man gave an artist no further scope for rich colour schemes or imposing decorative settings. Faced with the dreary democratic jacket and monotonous trousers, Perov rightly avoided them, and made the face, movement, and expression in his portraits all-important, sometimes the hands (as with Dostoyevsky), and he used a limited scale of sober grey or reddish brown colours. We are told that before he started to paint one of his Moscow portraits he travelled to Petersburg, in order to refresh his memory of the Van Dyck and Velasquez portraits in the Hermitage. He never lost his loyalty and reverence for Masters greater than himself, and never ceased to learn from them.

Perov's last but least successful phase was when he turned, under some official pressure, to try his hand at historical pictures, imbued with a strong patriotic flavour – like *The Pugachev Rebellion* – or to standard religious themes, like *Christ in the Garden of Gethsemane*. With pain and labour he forced himself to adopt epic poses and stale theological conventions, but he could put little or no heart into such artificial work, and the results were correspondingly poor.

In 1863 thirteen painters and one sculptor had rebelled against the Academy by flatly refusing to accept the latter's chosen subject for the annual Gold Medal competition. The rebels merely demanded the right to choose a subject for themselves, but the Academy insisted on their painting a single stilted theme, *The Banquet of the Gods in Valhalla*. The rebel artists managed to form a new cooperative group, which led to the foundation in 1870 of the *Society for Travelling Art Exhibitions*, the so-called *Peredvizhniki* (Travellers). The revolt was symptomatic. The better Russian artists simply refused to be confined any longer in the straitjacket which the out-of-date Academy imposed on them, in the shape of perfunctory and boring themes, selected from remote classical or Scandinavian mythology, to be presented as noble and morally instructive subjects.

Though Perov took part in the activities of this new society, its leader and moving spirit was I. Kramskoy (1837–87), a man of humble origin, whose mother was a Cossack married to a clerk in the town council of Ostrogorsk. At the age of fifteen, Kramskoy had been apprenticed to an icon painter, but remained with him only a few months. Then a travelling photographer, whose retoucher had disappeared on a drunken spree, engaged the young Kramskoy in 1853. For three years he methodically retouched photographs and painted them in colours. In 1857 he became a student at the Academy, and in 1860 his painting *Death of the Wounded Lensky* won him the Second Silver Medal.

When in 1863 he resigned in protest against the Academy's order to paint the *Banquet of the Gods in Valhalla*, he started to organize the *Peredvizhniki*. In one sense this revolt was bad for healthy art. For though it encouraged artists to abandon one stale academic convention, it drove them to embrace another modern utilitarian one, infected with a similar rigid zeal. Both old and new conventions were obsessed with the all-importance of socially edifying subject-matter. Talent, expressive skill, and inward spiritual quality, hardly concerned them, or escaped their notice. Kramskoy asserted, rather bluntly, to justify himself, that unless an artist's work can prove itself useful to human society, those exotic plants, called paintings, will no longer be able to blossom, since the demand for them will cease. This implicit identification of *useful* art with pictures of topical social grievances was, of course, an echo of the puritanical Chernyshevsky, but it remained a baleful criterion for the satisfaction of deeper human emotional needs. Apart from a few rather strained religious paintings, Kramskoy's own work consisted chiefly of portraits, in some of which he showed considerable interpretative skill, though without ever reaching the highest rank. His well-known portrait of the middle-aged Leo Tolstoy is one of his best efforts.

A more innately religious painter was Nicolas Gé (1831–94), a widely travelled experimentalist, who in 1882 became a fervent disciple of Tolstoy. His painfully human representations of a wretched or bewildered Christ shocked the Orthodox Church, and one of his paintings *What is Truth* (1890) was withdrawn from exhibition as blasphemous. Gé's blend of detailed, almost photographic, realism with tortured melodrama expressed a familiar modern predicament in art, but he failed to find any more satisfying solution. M. Nesterov (1862–1942) painted Orthodox religious subjects in a more sentimental and deliberately illustrative manner.

While the crudely indignant or gloomy narrative of the *Peredvizhniki* kept its grip on many artists, the continued search for an individually national style led to a refreshing artistic rediscovery of the Russian past. Already in the reign of Nicolas I the Government lavishly sponsored that research into neglected Russian art history which emerged in the folio volumes, *Antiquities of the Russian Empire*, richly illustrated with coloured lithographs. Archaeological societies were founded in Petersburg (1846) and Moscow (1864). The revived interest in old Russian religious painting kept pace with intensified architectural learning. D. A. Rovinsky (1824–95) started the systematic study, not only of icon painting, but also of Russian secular portraits and engravings. His work was carried further by a series of richly illustrated iconographic studies by N. P. Kondakov (1844–1925) and N. P. Likachev (1862–1935), who together established clear and convincing principles of connoisseurship for the first important historical collections of Russian and Greek icons, then in process of formation.

A still more comprehensive work was begun under the editorship of Igor Grabar (b. 1871), who published in 1909 the first volume of a complete history of Russian art and architecture, with sections contributed by leading archaeologists and art historians of the day. This monumental work, interrupted by the Revolution and two world wars, is still being brought up to date under careful Soviet supervision.

A more self-conscious revival of pre-Petrine Russian architecture was inaugurated in the reign of Alexander II with the building of the Historical Museum in Moscow (1874–83) by an architect of English origin, N. Sherwood. In religious architecture the lure of the sixteenth century was illustrated by A. Parland's *Church of the Resurrection* (1883), built in blatant imitation of Moscow's St Basil, on the spot in Petersburg where Alexander II had been murdered in 1881.

The painter most intimately connected with this phase of emotional Slavic revival was the vigorous Siberian, V. Surikov (1858–1916). Descendant of an old Cossack family, Surikov incorporated both the patriarchal traditions, brought to Siberia by the pioneer Yermak, and the sturdy independence cherished by many political exiles there. He managed to combine contemporary 'social criticism' with the nostalgic appeal of epoch-making scenes drawn from stirring events in national history. His most famous painting, *The Boyarinya Morozova* (Plate 121), on which he worked for three years (1881–3), represents a celebrated *Old Believer* being dragged through the streets to prison, in an open cart. Though it is a 'literary' picture, it conjured up with powerful exactitude the atmosphere of old Moscow, in a vital historical moment of acute conflict between personal religion and the expanding temporal power.

The whole gamut of human emotions is conveyed through the part played by individual figures in the scene; fear, idle curiosity, pity, anger, thoughtfulness, malicious mockery, and respect for stoic self-sacrifice. Every figure in the crowd is expressively alive, from the vindictive toothless priest mocking at the condemned 'heretic', the indifferent or laughing children, down to the ragged beggar, sitting in the snow, with his hand outstretched in deeply sympathetic benediction.

But the social commentary lies in the historic fact that this unashamedly 'literary' but compelling picture represents the personal revolt of a brave aristocratic lady, for the sake of her religious faith, her defiance of a spiritually crushing though nominally reformist State. Apart from the dramatic subject, and the skilful group composition, the painting of the gloomy grey sky, the heavy snow, and the cold reflected light on diverse human faces, render admirably the mood and character of a Russian winter scene.

V. Vereshchagin (1842–1904) was the only topical Russian artist who acquired international fame abroad during his lifetime. He specialized in vivid journalistic pictures of contemporary war scenes (especially from the Russo-Turkish War of 1877, in which he took part), bringing out the hideous horror, carnage and futility of modern war, to drive home his pacifist Tolstoyan message. He explained that he only wanted to make irrefutable facts speak for themselves on canvas. Cruel pictures of corpses and wounded soldiers lying abandoned on a grim battlefield, and about to be devoured by vultures, struck a compelling note, which stirred torpid public feeling in many countries. Such pictures were widely publicized and exhibited in the West, including Paris, London, and New York. Vereshchagin also painted a number of scenes, illustrating the Russian campaign against Napoleon in 1812. Despite his fame, he lived in a constant struggle with poverty. He owes his survival, as a leading artist, not to these many narrative pictures, but rather to the striking and sensitive portraits which he made of characteristic Eastern types, encountered during his extensive travels in the Caucasus, Central Asia, and India (Plate 127).

I. Repin (1844–1930), a man of humble origin, passed through the Academy, and became famous overnight for his picture *The Bargemen* (1870), more widely known as *The Volga Boatmen*, which was exhibited in Vienna in 1873. As a portraitist, Repin was indefatigable, but surprisingly uneven. He painted most of the famous writers, musicians, scientists, and statesmen of his day. He knew how to obtain both a speaking likeness and a bold dramatic effect. He handled strong and brilliant colours with a sure sense of tone values, though they could, when they passed out of control, become shockingly harsh and garish. One of his artistically most perfect portraits is that of the composer, M. Mussorgsky (1881), a subject who clearly inspired him to give his best (Plate 128).

After his visits to Paris in 1875 and 1883, Repin's work became more *impressionistic* in sensitive renderings of light, and his brushwork showed a discriminating avoidance of superfluous realistic detail. Some of his excursions into historical painting were considerably cruder than his portraits, but they won for him wider popular acclaim. His *Ivan IV with the Body of his Son* (1881) became a favourite with the Russian public, partly for its horrific sensational subject, and even more for its apparent protest against an autocratic crime. But the picture is painted in a coarsely melodramatic manner. Ivan, with a frenzied gesture, tries to check the stream of blood flowing from the wound of the son whom he has murdered. Other pictures by Repin, though they followed the fashion of moral commentary on current social events, rank much higher as pure narrative painting. His *They did not expect Him* (1883) depicts a released political prisoner unexpectedly entering the room where his family is sitting. The whole scene is ably composed and sensitively painted, with gentle interior lighting; it conveys an atmosphere of strong but mixed emotions stirring the human group.

V. Serov (1865–1911), son of a leading musician, grew up in highly civilized cosmopolitan circles, and continued his artistic education in Munich and Paris. A pupil of Repin, he developed more elegance and refinement than his master, and came closer to the mature manner of the French Impressionists. His *Portrait of Vera Mamontov* (1887) (Plate 130) reminds one of Renoir at his best, yet it is remarkable that Serov never saw any of Renoir's paintings till some years later. The painting shows a girl in a pink blouse, sitting at a table covered with a tablecloth, in a room flooded with soft light. On the table lie a few peaches, whose velvety tones match the colour of the girl's face. The picture is full of air, light, and a palpitating warmth. Here undoubtedly Serov made a big step forward, and found in everyday life a mysterious elusive beauty which his master, Repin, could not grasp. He was only twenty-two when he painted this masterpiece.

Serov excelled in the variety of his portraits, and never fell into the pitfalls of a stereotyped style. Even his official portraits have sincere informal character. His study of Nicolas II (1900) shows the Tsar absorbed in daily work, sitting thoughtfully at his desk. Without any grey official chill, the melancholy dark eyes and insignificantly handsome features of the ill-fated monarch come faithfully to life. In his portrait of M. Morozov (1902) (Plate 131B) Serov put into the figure of this ugly, thick-set, bald-headed millionaire his intimate knowledge of the vigorous upstart *nouveau riche*. Even his ill-fitting black frock-coat and smart trousers are not painted as mere status symbols of the successful bourgeois, but are crumpled in a characteristic manner by the impatient wearer. Serov's portrait of the great singer Chaliapin (1905) (Plate 131A) conveys the pathos of grand style as well as complex personal character, and his Anna Pavlova (1909) (Plate 132) captures for a moment the ethereal but steely grace of that unique and indefinably beautiful dancer.

Though little attracted by historical themes, Serov in his last years worked on his own interpretation of Peter the Great, whom he depicted as an abnormal human dynamo, a giant deformity, striding through his half-finished northern capital, possessed by a devil, and terrorizing all round him. He also loved drawing animals, especially horses, and did a whole series of illustrations for Krylov's Fables (1895–1905). Tending to misanthropy, he used to say that he now found animals more attractive, cheerful, and better subjects than boring contemporary human beings. A master of lighting effects, unconstrained composition, above all of intimate psychological portrayal, it seems all the more strange that he never painted perfectly the rounded shape of a human forehead and that the hands in his portraits were nearly always insensitive and sketchy. But he plumbed the depths of personality in a uniquely talented and individualist age, which was burning itself out in a dazzling outburst of uncoordinated human energy and brilliance.

M. Vrubel (1856–1910), born in Omsk, son of a Polish officer in the Russian army, and a half-Danish mother, brought a many-sided and exacting character to survey the Russian scene. Haunted by a conviction of modern European decline, which Russia was bound to share, he felt that he had deserved to be born in a more enlightened age. 'Are we not aware that the age of Michelangelo, Leonardo, even of Reynolds, has long since passed away, and that the mental level of our present-day artists has fallen astonishingly low?' he complained. But though he was surrounded by coarse or feebly decadent painters, he never sank to their level or fell a victim to soulless experiments and fashionable commercial mannerisms.

He entered the Academy in 1880, where he felt himself, like Serov, an international European, out of place among provincial Russian artists, obsessed with narrow nationalist or utilitarian clichés. In 1883 he was invited to supervise the restoration of the ancient Kirilov church in Kiev, and threw himself with ardour into the spirit of monumental Byzantine mosaics, a style to which he felt instinctively attracted. But his own efforts to work in this manner were strained and sketchy. He confessed that in our time true religious art had become such a helpless effort, so remote from the cold facts of our hurried and nervous mechanized life, that it must always seek outside support by reverting to archaeology or conscientious period imitation. But his intense study of assembling decorative particles in a glowing and expressive pattern found original fulfilment in a portrait which he painted at this time: *Young Girl against the Background of a Persian Carpet* (Plate 133), a composition full of mystery and charm, and executed in a masterly manner which does not date, being equally ancient and contemporary.

After he returned from Venice, where the surviving Byzantine frescoes and mosaics impressed him infinitely more than the glorious High Renaissance painters, he started to work on a series of illustrations for Lermontov's epic poem, *The Demon*. The mystic, religious strain in Vrubel's nature drew him to this theme, and he lived up to his ascetic part by inhabiting a single bare room, furnished only with two stools and an iron bed.

It was Vrubel's chief misfortune, and that of the late nineteenth-century Russian artists as a whole, that he never found a truly enlightened friend and patron. While State patronage remained academic or vulgarly patriotic, the rich industrialists were inclined to prefer frankly banal or frivolous 'modern' art. Both seemed frightened of serious, rare and sensitive talent, which either escaped their notice or was barely tolerated. Few cultured independent-minded patrons had survived, and Emancipation had crippled the economic power of the former art-loving aristocracy. A talent like Vrubel's therefore became a voice crying in the wilderness, even as other voices, sweeter and stronger, had cried before, seeking firm support and sympathy in vain.

In 1889 Vrubel moved to Moscow, where he executed a number of commissions for the wealthy merchant, S. Mamontov. It was an unhealthy symptom of the times that an artist, who ought to have been cherished by his compatriots like a rare creative force, was obliged to paint the walls of a private theatre, to decorate the gaudy ostentatious mansion of a Moscow merchant, or draw experimental cubist designs on the back of a *balalaika*. He could not in his poverty refuse even such a trivial employment of his talent. Yet Vrubel never yielded to self-pity, nor did he sink into that empty Bohemian dissipation so dear to frustrated second-rate artists of his day.

In 1896 he married an opera singer, and thus became drawn into the world of theatrical costume and stage design. He still strenuously shunned artistic cliques and their soul-destroying intellectual jargon, and himself rarely and unwillingly talked about art. He became intensely absorbed in his work on Lermontov's *Demon*, feverishly repainting his sinister principal figure, and even doing a separate version of it in terracotta sculpture, in order to paint it again, after having thereby gained a surer sense of three-dimensional form (Plate 134). He had become obsessed with the relentless destructive power of evil dominating the modern world. The blatant petty vulgarity of those around him preyed upon his mind. He felt forced to fritter away his energy in fighting people who dragged him down into the dust, when 'art with all its power tries to provide illusions for the soul, to wake it from everyday trivialities by invoking majestic images'. Having failed to sell his picture, *The Demon*, to the Tretyakov Gallery, he exhibited it in Petersburg in 1901. He kept on running into the gallery to retouch and improve the painting, even after the exhibition was already open to the public.

In 1902 Vrubel became mentally ill. Overstrain, ill-health, and perpetual frustration had driven him to breaking-point. But he continued to work in lucid intervals, often returning to his earlier Byzantine manner. He made numerous drawings and water-colours on religious themes, a favourite one being St John the Baptist. His portrait of the symbolist poet, V. Bryusov, which later won him acclaim abroad for its geometrical modernity and cubist touch, now seems more remarkable for its static strength and psychological penetration (Plate 135). Russia had received Vrubel like a wandering minstrel, to whom it gave a night's lodging, food and wine, in return for the fleeting entertainment with which he provided them. But his patrons failed to understand his aims or to give him the scope and type of encouragement which he deserved. A first-class draughtsman, a more sincere visionary than any of his contemporaries, he was genuinely carried away by visual dreams of a greater invisible world. Some called him a decadent psychopath, a victim of hallucinations, without stopping to observe that his unconventionally religious nature had always hated and opposed the coarsely decadent strains invading both Western and Russian painting at this time. He could more justly be deemed a victim of unbalanced emotions and of an ungrateful Philistine environment, which denied him that deeper fulfilment in his work, through which both he and they might have derived more lasting spiritual benefit.

For Russian art, throughout this crucial period, seems to have been tortured and torn by three mutually incompatible endeavours – the craving to develop a *national* style, the struggle to maintain higher international standards of taste and achievement, inherited from the past, and the fashionable desire to be considered up-to-date and abreast of western Europe. While the first sank easily into bogus pictorial chauvinism, the second tended to peter out in rigid academic 'set pieces', while the third produced poor imitations of the sicklier, more ephemeral, modern European movements.

At the same time there was already growing in the educated class a strong reaction against that perfunctory national topicality and clumsy styleless realism which dominated the 1870s. A finer taste was awakening in Russia, a stronger appreciation of that haunting past grace and beauty which the prosaic radicals

were busily destroying. A brighter flame flared up for the last time before it died
out. That revival, whether inspired by eighteenth-century Petersburg or by
pre-Petrine Moscow, undoubtedly stimulated all the arts in Russia. It centred,
in painting, round the powerful but enigmatic figure of Serge Diaghilev (1872–
1929).

Diaghilev became the moving spirit of that group of artists and writers, called
The World of Art, and he founded a journal of that name in 1898. It lasted until
1905, when its editorial board provided the unofficial committee which organized
the huge historical exhibition of Russian portrait painting, opened at the Tauride
Palace in that year. *The World of Art* was succeeded by a more *avant-garde*
journal, *The Golden Fleece,* which in its snobbish efforts to be up to date, feebly
succumbed to the pretentious -isms of Parisian post-impressionists. Two other
twentieth-century Petersburg journals *Stariye Gody* (Old Years) and *Stolitsa i
Usad'ba* (The Capital and the Country House), showed a nostalgic desire to learn
from the art and architecture of a vanishing Russia. In 1906 Diaghilev organized
an exhibition of Russian art in Paris, and in the following year he presented
Mussorgsky's *Boris Godunov* at the Paris opera. The boldly brilliant sets and
costumes were designed by the Russian artists, Benois and Golovin. In this way
Diaghilev started to release a mighty exodus of Russian talent to the pleasantly
astonished West.

Initial success encouraged him to launch a far more ambitious undertaking, his
Ballets Russes, which he brought to the Châtelet Theatre, Paris, in 1909. This
event took the French capital by storm. Critics, artists, aristocrats, and bourgeoisie,
all raved about it, all found it equally fascinating and vital. Here was a gorgeous
vibrating Renaissance of dancing and music, allied with visual art, gently caressing
the starved senses and blunted nerves, bubbling and overflowing with wholly
unexpected colour, light, rhythm, and enchanting harmony. For Diaghilev had
freed from its gilded coffin the mummified Russian Imperial ballet, miraculously
preserved like some gorgeous fossilized insect in layers of amber, but safe
from the common decay which had corrupted that same art form in the West.
He woke the *Sleeping Princess* from her bewitched slumber and brought her back
to Europe.

One French critic aptly pointed out that such a miraculously gifted company
could not possibly have been found or trained in Paris, or indeed in any 'democratic'
country, commercially dependent on providing standard entertainment suited to

XXV. A MOSCOW TEA-HOUSE. V. Kustodiev, late 19th century.

the average urban public. The crowd, he noted, which fills our music halls, wants tumultuous noisy numbers, loud laughter or sexual excitement. They cannot share the pure devotion of the enthusiastic connoisseur. For Diaghilev's ballets, with all their passionate vitality, had a delicate exotic flavour, appealing rather to the vivid imaginative taste of a cultivated but not yet blasé aristocracy. They stood for a momentary spiritual triumph, perhaps the last of its kind, over a triumphant onslaught of the trivial, slovenly, or fraudulent.

Yet even a frankly commercial showman, like J. B. Cochran, paid tribute to the overwhelming superiority of Diaghilev's art to profitable 'leg-shows', when he proclaimed: 'Were the world run on the right lines, Diaghilev would be appointed international Minister of Culture by all the countries in the world whose taste he has improved, and to whom he has brought such an abundance of refreshing beauty by his Russian ballets.'

Diaghilev's starting-point was undiluted disgust with the intolerable provincial philistinism of his self-satisfied compatriots, and his own firm refusal to be bullied by the clumsy Russian bureaucracy. He believed strongly in the hidden or suppressed imaginative riches of his country, and he was determined to reveal them, both to herself and to the outside world, unduly preoccupied with the more sinister spectacle of Russian political entanglements. A man who dreamed of blending the right music with riotous colour and dramatic human movement, on a gorgeously lavish scale, but drilled with the steely precision of a tireless dictatorial will, he undoubtedly provided the joy of miraculous magic to multitudes who were sick of the cheap and tedious platitudes, dished up by entertainment-mongers of contemporary urban society.

The tremendous service rendered thus by Diaghilev was scantily appreciated by all but a few of his contemporaries, nor can it readily be grasped today by those who have never experienced the strange exhilaration of his ballets. Unfortunately, the painters, dancers, and musicians, drawn together and endowed with creative power under his compelling hypnotic touch, quickly disintegrated or dispersed after he had died.

It should be recalled that in the 1890s thwarted easel painters were growing hungry for a wider scope, which some found in fresco, but too few architects with taste and initiative emerged, to place at their disposal the large walls for which they craved. This paradoxical situation gave rise to a hybrid type of picture, rather sketchily painted, like a fresco, for a broad effect, and called a panel. It is not surprising that the painters' struggle for imaginative décor on a bigger scale found a more satisfying outlet in the theatre, most of all in scenery and costume for opera and ballet. If in a grossly irreligious age no chance was left to attain the grandiose permanence of Byzantine wall painting, the artist of our day could at least hope to become *Caliph for an hour*, enthroned among the ephemeral cardboard palaces of the stage.

N. Roerich (1874–1947) became an ambitious large-scale painter of this kind, who found fruitful theatrical opportunities with the help of Diaghilev. But while the majority of the *Mir Iskusstva* group hankered after the gallant age of French rococo or the elegant decadence of eighteenth-century Venice, the vision of Roerich was fixed on a remote pre-Moscow pagan Russia, a legendary Scandinavia, or medieval Europe. There is a stern, broad, and concentrated vigour in his designs for the Polovtsian camp in the ballet, *Prince Igor*, and for the vaulted monastery in Maeterlinck's *Sister Beatrice*. But his conception of primeval Russia found a unique outlet in sets for *Le Sacre du Printemps*, in which Stravinsky's weird music and Nijinsky's genius as a dancer combined hitherto untried patterns of movement, sound and visual ritual. Here the pre-Christian Slav world uncovered the timeless face of elemental human beings, moved by an innocent modest awe in front of nature's impenetrable mysteries.

Later Roerich set himself up as a theosophist, and managed to persuade some kindly Americans, susceptible to the charm of eloquent mystics, to endow a museum in his name in New York. The same supporters financed in 1924 a Central Asian Expedition, which he headed (recorded in *Trails to Inmost Asia*, Yale University Press, 1931). His pictorial output was prodigious, and the New York Museum alone contains over a thousand paintings by him. But the modern visitor is soon wearied by such a plethora of bare rocks, cardboard mountains, and dreamlike clouds. Roerich intrigued his followers still more when he bought a house in Tibet and lived for a time in solitude among the mountain peaks. In 1928 he became director of a Himalayan Research Institute, which had a base in the Punjab, and he also promoted a new Centre of Art and Culture at Allahabad. His son carried on his work in northern India.

But the painters to whom Diaghilev gave creative opportunities were mostly aesthetic eclectics, who looked back to the cosmopolitan grandeur of Catherine the Great's grandee art patrons, to the harmonious elegance of Alexander I's Petersburg, in order to stir their sluggish modern imagination into action.

It was partly to *Russianized* foreigners of the eighteenth century that Russians themselves owed the birth of their vital modern art. The acute nostalgia of their descendants proved rich in valuable re-discoveries. A. Benois, himself of mixed French and Italian descent, awoke his compatriots to the nearly forgotten splendours of eighteenth-century Petersburg, and to the superb portraits of Levitsky and Borovikovsky. On the other hand, the *World of Art* rarely inspired its adherents to original and serious painting of their own. Most of them preferred, like K. Somov, to move along a smoother path, and found pleasure in the lighter media suited to their taste, the gouache, water-colour, or pen-and-ink drawing, where they allied a graceful sensuality with pure but tenuous romantic feeling.

A. Benois (1870–1961), though never a pure painter, developed into a first-class illustrator and stage decorator, whose exquisite water-colour sketches and drawings, for costume and scenery, hold a place of their own in the history of theatrical decoration. Perhaps his greatest creation (under Diaghilev's guidance) was the ballet *Petrushka*, a *tour de force* of Slavic urban folk-lore, in which his scenic art was reinforced by Stravinsky's haunting dramatic music. His multifarious activity as designer, art-critic, editor and writer, used up his abundant creative energy.

Two minor stars of this group, A. Golovin (b. 1863), and K. Korovin (b. 1861), both found their feet solely as theatrical artists. The theatre drew painters to it, absorbed them and sometimes ate them up, but it enabled them to serve a clear temporary purpose in a restless unstable age, when highly finished easel paintings were being described as a superfluous anachronism. Seen at close quarters, these stage décor paintings looked hurried, coarse and garish, but at a distance, mellowed by skilful artificial lighting, they created the desired illusion.

M. Dobujinsky (1884–1958) felt more at home in designing *period pieces* for the stage than in the agitated world of ballet. His style was clever, elegant, but coldly formal, and he rarely got beyond the technique and outlook of a highly competent book illustrator. His talents found most adequate expression in the charming period sets which he designed for Turgenev's play *A Month in the Country*, produced by the Moscow Art Theatre (Plate 137).

Boris Kustodiev (1878–1933), grandson of a priest, became a masterly genre painter of Russian provincial life and of the more picturesque features of the urban merchant class environment. His depth and range of talent outstripped and enlivened his humdrum subject-matter. He joined the *Mir Iskusstva* group, and in 1903 spent a year studying in Paris. Apart from his strong flair for local character, he could achieve the most luminous and buoyant colour harmonies, and it is significant that his own favourite old Master was the gorgeous Tintoretto. As well as contributing something decidedly robust and individual both to genre painting and stage décor, he was one of the few brilliantly successful colourists among the Russian artists of that generation, though today he is almost forgotten (Plate XXV).

S. Soudeikin, with his gaily coloured cubist dolls, N. Goncharova, with her stylized fairy-tale and neo-Slav architectural designs for the ballet based on Rimsky-Korsakov's *Le Coq d'Or* (1914), M. Chagall, with his fashionable, light, and whimsical fantasies, were all essentially *artistes décorateurs*. A. Yakovlev, though he produced stage scenery for the *Moscow Art Theatre*, later went beyond it, and in emigration painted strikingly powerful studies of African and Asiatic types, whom he encountered during his distant travels.

That impassioned exoticism, at once semi-barbaric and sophisticated, which permeated the *World of Art* group, found its brightest exponent in Léon Bakst (1868–1924). A pupil of the Imperial Academy in 1890, he announced that the great age of Pericles had been vulgarized, debased and enervated by every official Academy in Europe. Academies no longer helped vital art, but did everything they could to kill it, by making easy and corrupt compromises in a sphere where compromise was a sin against the Holy Ghost. Here Bakst found an unexpected ally in the veteran art critic, V. Stasov, who finally condemned the Petersburg Academy when, not content with debasing classical standards, it started to flirt with decadent modern cliques. 'There are limits,' he fulminated. 'One does not display in a public exhibition paralysed people, epileptics, victims of infectious diseases. Let the decadents exist, but don't let them show off their grimaces and deformities in the Academy! Our unstable youth, its mind already clouded by false slogans about "new art", will now be able to exclaim: "Look, the Academy applauds them, presses them to its heart!"' (*Decadents in the Academy*, February 1901).

After the Russian Revolution, Bakst went off on an independent voyage of exploration to Greece. Here the flowing linear rhythms of early vase painting inspired him to start his own work again. He stepped backwards from the more familiar Athens of Pericles into the deeper mysteries of archaic Greece, having already tasted the 'spiced poison' of the East. Bakst remained a brave artist, who, in the grimly mechanized times through which we live, dared to revive the distant past in order to rediscover the lost and prostituted human soul in a realm of myth and virgin forests.

A natural eclectic, and a stage wizard, Bakst conjured up his scenic decoration from an abundance of diverse historical epochs. He could rise to an orgiastic riot of oriental colour in such ballets as *Cleopatra* and *Shéherazade*. He could equally well echo and adapt the crisp gay vibrations of Greek Vase ornament (in décor for the plays of Sophocles and the ballet *Narcissus*) (Plate 136). But he was also at home in the dreamily romantic kingdom of lace crinolines and sweetly scented fading bouquets (in Schumann's *Carnaval* and Weber's *Le Spectre de la Rose*).

Sharp, bold, and astonishing blends of seemingly contradictory styles, enriched with an exotic flavour, were characteristic of Bakst. He brought to a brilliant climax that adventurous revivalist movement, which made the theatre more glowingly pictorial than it had ever been before, but also obliged painting to grow whole-heartedly theatrical. This fruitful marriage of two allied arts undoubtedly revitalized the theatre, ballet, and opera. And it provided a stimulating new outlet for a whole generation of easel painters, who were stricken by uncertainty about how to find a worthy place and purpose for their imaginative work in a noisily chaotic and increasingly technical environment.

117. THE MAJOR'S COURTSHIP. P. Fedotov, 1848. *Russian Museum, Leningrad.*

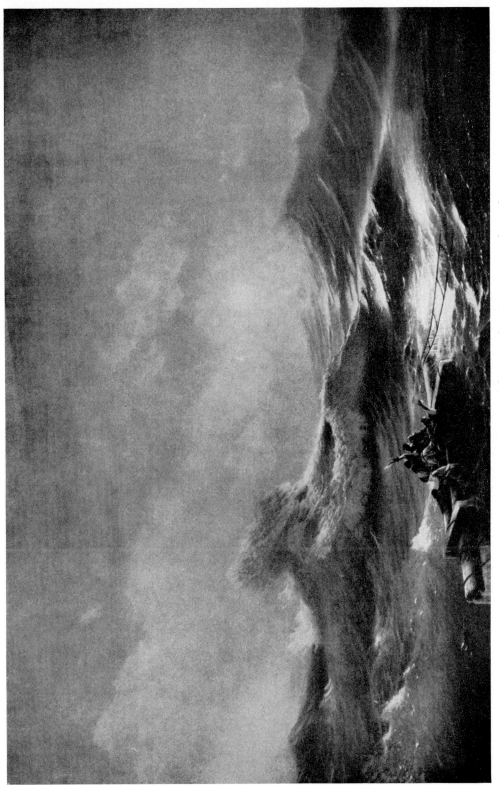

118A. THE NINTH WAVE. I. Ayvazovsky. *Russian Museum, Leningrad.*

119. FOUNTAINS IN THE GARDEN OF PETERHOF, built for Peter the Great. From an early 19th century water-colour.
Collection, G. Talbot Esq., Tunbridge Wells, England.

120. VIEW OF THE PASHKOV HOUSE, later the Rumyantsev Museum, now part of the Lenin Library, Moscow. From an early 19th century engraving.

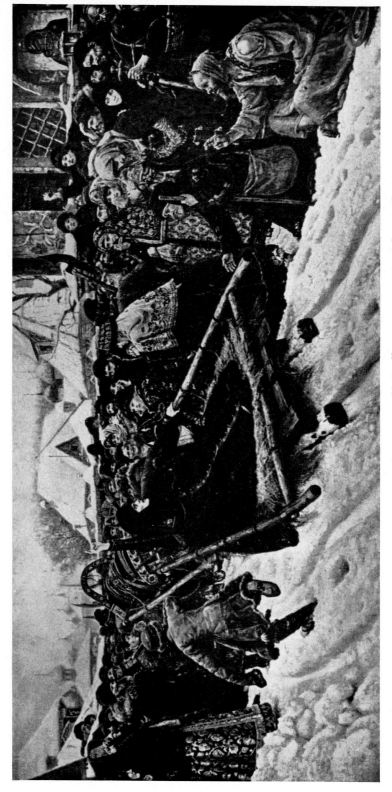

121. THE BOYARINYA MOROZOVA. V. Surikov, c. 1882. *Tretyakov Gallery.*

122. ON THE BOULEVARD. V. G. Makovsky. *Tretyakov Gallery.*

123. THE RAVENS HAVE ARRIVED. A. Savrasov, 1871. *Tretyakov Gallery.*

124A. PEASANT GIRL
carrying a basket of
cabbages. Water-colour.
A. Stryelkovsky, dated 1856.
Private Collection, London.

124B. GYPSY GIRL.
A. Harlamov. Mid-
19th century.

125. THE VILLAGE FUNERAL. V. Perov, 1865. *Tretyakov Gallery.*

126. THE TEA DRINKING. V. Perov, 1862. *Tretyakov Gallery.*

127. A MOHAMMEDAN SERVANT. V. Vereshchagin, late 19th century. *Tretyakov Gallery*.

128. THE COMPOSER, M. MUSSORGSKY. I. Repin, 1881. *Tretyakov Gallery.*

129. PEASANT BOY IN A VILLAGE SCHOOL. N. Bogdanov-Byelsky, late 19th century. *Molotov Art Gallery*.

130. VERA MAMONTOV. V. Serov, 1887. *Tretyakov Gallery.*

131A. THE YOUNG F. CHALIAPIN. V. Serov, 1905. Former
collection of Moscow Literary Artistic Circle.

131B. M. MOROZOV. V. Serov, 1887.
Tretyakov Gallery.

132. SKETCH OF ANNA PAVLOVA. V. Serov, 1909. Late 19th century. Former collection of A. Botkin, Petersburg.

134. THE DEMON. Painted terracotta sculpture. M. Vrubel, 1890. Former collection of A. Botkin, Petersburg.

(*facing page*)

133. GIRL AGAINST THE BACKGROUND OF A PERSIAN CARPET. M. Vrubel. Former collection of I. Tereshchenko.

135. THE POET, V. BRYUSOV. M. Vrubel. Former collection of M. Ryabushinsky.

136. Sketch of a costume for Cherapin's ballet *Narcissus*. L. Bakst, early 20th century.

137. Design for a scene in Turgenev's play *A Month in the Country*. M. Dobujinsky, early 20th century.

XXVI. (*top to bottom*) Old man playing a guitar. Man and woman playing cards.
Tradesman with his apprentice. Girl carrying buckets of water on a yoke.
Painted paper mâché boxes by Lukutin Factory, mid- and late 19th century.

CHAPTER SEVEN

Some Distinctive Russian Decorative Arts

Russian peasant art, though it became endowed with a mystic but confusing sanctity by a few educated revivalists in the nineteenth century, remained primarily that simple spontaneous art which had arisen in the distant past from the peasant's traditional mode of life. It embraced his modest wooden hut, it beautified his hand-made tools and household goods, his clothes and means of transport. Apart from textiles, its main material was wood, potter's clay or bone, expressed in the form of carved eaves and window-frames, carved panels of scenes from the life of Christ (Plate 139A), boat-shaped drinking-vessels (Plate 138), toy animals and birds, decorative combs, or gaily painted spinning-wheels.

Tolstoy admired this art, because, though relatively static, it clearly satisfied the healthy imaginative needs of hard-working agricultural people, not yet infected by the more prosperous but restless townsman's morbid craving for any and every trivial novelty. Peasant art remained sincere, nor was it frightened to repeat itself, because, in so doing, it need not grow stale. If it had no history and underwent no basic change, that may have been because it felt instinctively that happy people need no history. But it knew how to reveal fresh personal and local variations on every important time-honoured theme. Even the endless painted representations of the joyfully dashing peasant *troika* never identically repeat themselves, nor do the decorative wooden arches, hung with tinkling bells, over the horses' necks.

Unfortunately Tolstoy and the *narodnik* idealists drew absurdly far-fetched conclusions about the modern peasant's noble and gifted nature, derived from the precarious survival in our time of a vigorous but ancient peasant art. It might be reasonable to claim, as Tolstoy did, that a peasant with unperverted taste could judge better the kind of art which *he needed* than any urban intellectual judging what he *ought* to like. But it was far-fetched to attribute a monopoly of imaginative and moral virtues to the nebulous *collective soul*, whatever that entity might be, of the Russian common people in their blessed ignorance. There could be a wonderful and timeless beauty in the best traditional peasant songs and dances. But it was an

251

138. KOVSCH (drinking vessel) carved in wood, with stylized horses' heads. Made in the Tver province, early 19th century. *State Historical Museum, Moscow.*

ominous fact that nineteenth-century peasants already felt far less drawn towards that magnetic beauty than did members of the educated class, who now longed to keep it pure and undefiled, and did all they could to save the modern peasants from succumbing to the uglier vices rampant in an urbanized industrial society.

And while educated Russians craved for an influx of fresh unadulterated blood from an agricultural *Arcadia*, to cure their oversophisticated art of its 'advanced' anaemia, peasant art itself had been profoundly modified by the dominating taste of aristocratic landowners and vigorous townspeople throughout the eighteenth and nineteenth centuries. Both subject-matter and approach had widely changed. Noble heraldic emblems, classical garlands, gorgeous carriages and elegant costumes, had invaded the realm of age-old geometrical or stylized shapes and patterns. Elaborate carving in wood or ivory (Plates 139B, 140, 151), painted wood

252

and papier mâché, chasing and engraving metal, ceramics, embroidery, weaving and lace (among textiles the most conservative in design), all continued to reflect the religious and domestic taste of peasant craftsmen, but increasingly permeated by the strong imagination of their educated masters, who persistently trained and employed them in building and decorating innumerable churches and country houses.

Not only did the peasant artist become more versatile at this time, developing a wider range both of subjects and of artistic skill, but he began to see himself in a mellower light. A genuine admiration and interest from above seemed to rejuvenate his own creative powers, and started to enliven formal or stereotyped peasant symbolism. Cosy scenes of tea-drinking round a table with a *samovar*, gay boys and girls dancing happily in green meadows, dreamy and gentle village maidens throwing garlands in the stream, *troikas* with eager friendly horses galloping madly across the snow-covered fields, colourful girl water-carriers, top-hatted shepherds rounding up a herd, all began to reflect in art the compelling charm of agreeably idealized peasant life, much more vividly than in any earlier age (Plates XXVI, XXVIII, XXXI, XXXII).

After the abolition of serfdom in 1861, and still more with the urban drift gathering momentum towards the end of the nineteenth century, all these peasant arts rapidly declined, as they had done in western Europe, and for similar economic reasons. Fine hand-made work could no longer compete in price with mass-produced factory products, and fewer people were prepared to pay for it, though plenty could have afforded to, had they so desired. The local authorities and a few enlightened landowners made sincere and strenuous efforts to keep Russian handicrafts alive, but they proved hardly more successful than such attempts had been in western industrialized countries. And the more sombre intelligentsia, probing into the problem with their analytic minds, failed to grasp that inviolable symbolic instinct which remained dear to the hearts of forcibly urbanized Russian common people.

In the early twentieth century Princess Tenisheva founded a craft centre on her estate at Talashkina. The millionaire merchant, S. Morozov, did the same at his country house, Abramtsevo. But the stimulus which they gave to a revival of ancient Russian style was short-lived, and suffered from a strained self-consciousness, an almost counterfeit artificiality. For too long educated Russians had been taught to regard peasant handicrafts with condescension, as some conventional, half-childish relic, a quaint archaic ethnographical genre. When this attitude changed abruptly in the nineteenth century, and swung over to the opposite extreme of *exalté* peasant-worship, it came too late to save a whole way of life already undermined by stark commercial greed and contempt for humble un-complaining poverty.

In fact, peasant art, serving exclusively the peasant's own domestic needs and tastes, and decorative arts, serving the Court, the Church and landowning nobility, had become two distinct currents, of which the latter underwent more foreign influence, but had also proved itself to be more varied and vigorous. Even basic peasant art, stimulated by French and German innovations, grew much more lively until the middle of the nineteenth century. Traditional lacquered peasant furniture, painted with bold and warmly coloured designs in red and gold, flourished at this time, and was extensively made for the homes of the wealthier classes (Plate 141). A few decades earlier, serf craftsmen, encouraged and trained by enterprising francophil masters, had managed to create remarkably fine native adaptations of French Louis XVI and Empire models, while using the most attractive Russian woods, like the golden blonde Karelian birch (Plates 143 and XXVIIA and B).

In the eighteenth and early nineteenth centuries, outstanding and distinctive furniture was made in Tula (famous for its *samovars*) by the local specialists in wrought iron and steel. These pieces, chiefly chairs, but also tables, and even fire-places for the European market, were of intricate and original design (Plates 142A and B). Later nineteenth-century Russian furniture showed less distinctive national character or style, unless it frankly copied seventeenth-century Muscovite or peasant models. Malachite mosaic tops and sumptuous gilding distinguished the more luxurious pieces, but the shapes remained essentially western European. A unique double-fronted chest, dated 1873, made in carved ebony, encrusted with floral scrolls in gilded bronze, is illustrated here (Plate 144). The bosses in the centre of each panel are carved out of solid blocks of *lapis lazuli*.

Crude and heavy Russian peasant pottery seems to have first broken its mono-tony during the eighteenth century, when it attained a striking artistic style in bold design and coloured glazes (Plate 145). The majolica technique, imported from the West, was developed at that time in the Gjelsk district, where the best pottery and china clay had been found. The designers were fond of representing human forms, wild flowers and domestic animals, especially cocks, hares, squirrels, and horses, with or without riders. Though ornament was rarely refined, it was

XXVIIA. (*facing, above*) Three chairs in Karelian birch, one with medallion bust of Alexander I, and his consort, in ormolu. *c.* 1810.

XXVIIB. (*facing, below*) Sofa in Karelian birch, with ormolu ornament. Petersburg, *c.* 1810.

always vigorous and worked out in keeping with the form, size, and purpose of the main object. In the nineteenth century, exactly the same decorative themes continued, but they grew more elongated and elaborate (Plate 146).

One of the most attractive and characteristically Russian arts, illustrating a highly creative collaboration between peasant craftsmen and the Westernized upper class, can be found in the papier mâché objects of utility, painted with fine miniatures, started in a small factory towards the end of the eighteenth century by an enlightened industrialist, called P. Korobov. Fedoskino, a village in the Krasnopolyansky region of the Moscow province, appears to have drawn together some hereditary painters. It was chosen by Korobov as the most suitable centre for his undertaking, at a time when the painting of icons had fallen into decline, but while gifted underemployed painters were still available. The first workshop was started in the neighbouring village of Danilkovo. Local talent switched over from sacred subjects to contemporary secular themes, and Korobov skilfully employed these adaptable artists to paint exquisite miniature scenes on snuffboxes, jewel-cases, blotters, and many other objects of utility.

The most remarkable thing about this enterprise was its rapid and complete success, both from the artistic and commercial standpoints. We learn from official records that in the year 1804 alone, 13,000 of these painted papier mâché objects were produced, of which about 9,000 were bought by Russians, as *objets d'art* which also aptly served a practical domestic use, while the remainder found a ready market in foreign countries. In the first quarter of the nineteenth century the factory passed into the ownership of Korobov's son-in-law, P. Lukutin. He initiated a still wider range of products, including boxes for needlework, cigarette-cases, match-boxes, trays, Easter eggs and pencil-holders (Plates XXVI, XXVIII, *et seq*).

The subjects chosen for most of the painted miniatures were characteristic scenes, drawn from peasant or middle-class daily life. Some displayed architectural views and a few chose historical figures or religious themes. Altogether they provide a fascinating cross-section of Russian social life and personal taste in the early nineteenth century. The compositions were mostly drawn from pre-existing models – a natural faculty for icon painters, accustomed to start from Byzantine prototypes. They now used chiefly oil-paintings, water-colours and engravings. The latter lent themselves, however, to free adaptation by the village painters, who endowed them with rich and glowing colour schemes, which were entirely the

artists' own creation. Though scrupulously observing formal rules and real subject-matter, like their icon-painting predecessors, they could also let their fertile
imagination run riot in gorgeous colour fantasies.

P. Roussel's well-known painting of a Russian dance-scene was frequently
adapted and simplified by the Lukutin miniature painters. Roussel depicted eleven
dancers, Lukutin only eight or fewer, of which two are dancing, while one plays the
balalaika and the rest look on. The artists constantly repeated with lively variations such typical scenes as *Return from the Harvest, Tea-Drinking, The Girl
Water-Carrier, Drunken Peasants, Driving in Troikas, Playing Cards,* cab-drivers,
balalaika-players, and street-vendors, in their picturesque professional costumes
(Plate XXVI). Favourite architectural ensembles were the Red Square, the Moscow
Kremlin seen across the river, and the lavishly barbaric Cathedral of St Basil
(Plate XXX).

The unique technical methods employed by these miniature painters, partly
derived from the old icon workshops, demanded a high degree of skill. They
applied three or four separate layers of thin paint in yolk of egg tempera, allowed
each coat to dry, and then covered them with transparent lacquer. That process
partly explains the secret of their exceptional purity and intense depth of colouring. But they also laid on the paint in two distinct manners, the so-called *opaque,*
to give intensity, and the *transparent,* for mellow brilliance. The latter aimed at
preserving, through several translucent layers of paint, the visibility of the metallic
or mother-of-pearl ground below. As had traditionally been done for icons, pure
gold leaf or silver powder were often applied to the surface of papier mâché objects
as basic grounds. Red pigments painted on the top, with gold shining through them,
and strong blue or green painted over shimmering silver, led to wonderful effects
of jewel-like glowing colour. The Lukutin artists also achieved a striking painted
imitation of tortoiseshell for the interiors of their boxes, and the quality of their
red lacquer rivalled that of the best Chinese or Japanese examples.

It is not surprising that P. Lukutin's unique products attracted widespread
admiration, and soon began to figure prominently in important Russian and
International Exhibitions. In 1828 he acquired from the Court the right to paint
the Imperial double-headed eagle in gold on all his authentic articles. That emblem
was accompanied either by the initial or full name of the Lukutin owner at the
time, or by the words 'Lukutin Factory', written in gold and shaped like the seg-
ment of a circle.

XXVIII. (*top to bottom*) Young Boyar and his Bride. Woman with a Spinning Wheel.
Young woman with two suitors and a dog. Painted papier mâché boxes.
Made by Lukutin, 19th century.

SOME DISTINCTIVE RUSSIAN DECORATIVE ARTS

M. Zagoskin, an observant Russian connoisseur, who travelled abroad in the mid-nineteenth century, wrote in his *Moscow and the Muscovites* (1842): 'Some of our artistic workshops can now without shame be compared with the best foreign European ones. The porcelain of Popov, the silver wares of Sazykov, would command a high place anywhere in France or England. I need hardly mention the factory of Lukutin, because relatively it stands higher than all the others. It is far superior to the celebrated Brunswick lacquer.' P. Korobov is said to have visited Brunswick in the eighteenth century, and studied there the local lacquer work, before he started his workshop in Danilkovo. Of various other small Russian factories, which began to make similar objects, only that of Vishnyakov survived competition with Lukutin. Though the two factories were almost identical in their choice of themes and objects, Vishnyakov was on the whole less refined in craftsmanship. The latter factory was largely staffed by ex-serf craftsmen of Count Sheremetyev, who had bought their freedom prior to 1861. Its mark is the name Vishnyakov, usually painted in a circle.

The son of P. Lukutin, N. Lukutin, carried on the family firm until the end of the 1880s. Though he managed to maintain the same high standard for discriminating individual orders, he felt financially compelled to steer the business into a larger output of cheap, artistically second-rate products, and of large-scale boxes, coarser and heavier in style, but more suited to the taste of the newly rich provincial commercial class. In 1904, after the death of the last Lukutin owner, and depressed by the outbreak of the Russo-Japanese war, the factory closed down. A number of its artists found alternative employment in painting metal tea-trays with bright floral bouquets and dashing *troikas*. These were also in demand for export. But in 1910, with the help of the Morozov Fund, and the local government council, a new co-operative *artel* was founded, with the name *Fedoskino Craftsmens' Guild of former artists of the Lukutin Factory*. This guild revived the output of lacquered boxes. In the same year it won a silver medal at an Arts and Crafts Exhibition in Kazan, and in 1913 it won a gold medal at a larger exhibition of that kind, held in Kiev.

The *Fedoskino Guild* received much-advertised support during the Soviet period, as the most important surviving centre of a unique and traditional Russian art. But its products, though similar, should not be identified with those from the villages of Palekh, Mstera, and Khouly. The latter, led by Palekh, a former centre for icon painters, have been supported by the Soviet authorities and played a larger part in the revival of Russian miniature painting, adapted to the special demands of a Soviet environment. Their artists can still paint the most delicately executed copies of charming nineteenth-century Russian oil-paintings by Venetsianov, Fedotov, Perov and other masters. But they have also introduced a lot of new, colourful, sometimes gaudily painted, themes, drawn from folklore, old Russian fairy-tales and Pushkin's narrative poems. These compete, rather oddly, with standard Soviet subjects, painted with all the hard didactic attributes of full-blown 'Socialist realism', *Lenin among the Children*, muscular *Heroes of Labour* and *Fighters for Peace*, performing their exemplary feats on the industrial or military battle-fronts.

Another special *genre*, inspired by idealized peasant life, developed in the small-scale bronze groups and figures, created throughout the nineteenth century. The more elaborate and sensitively modelled of these works were cast in gilded bronze and set on malachite stands, with splendid decorative effect (Plates 147 and 148A). A few resembled the graceful figures of national Russian types, made in the early nineteenth century for the Imperial and Gardner Porcelain factories. They show the same elegant restraint, finesse of modelling, and static quality. It is possible that some were cast from clay models made by artists who worked primarily on figures for the porcelain factories. Others, though more sentimental and literary in the late nineteenth-century manner, have an assured documentary style and crisp vitality, like the charming small-scale peasant groups in bronze, made by the well-known sculptor, E. A. Lanseré (1848–86) (Plate 148B), who also did Cossack figures, and may have done a small unsigned equestrian statue of Alexander II, in the uniform of a general in the Imperial Cossack Bodyguard Regiment (Plate 149).

Excellent and distinctive ivory carvings were also made throughout the nineteenth century, both in the traditional Archangel style (Plate 151), typical of that part of northern Russia, and in the more elaborate Westernized manner (Plate 150), developed for the Court and aristocratic patrons.

The Imperial Glass, Porcelain and Textile factories shared certain rare characteristics, now extinct. Since all three worked primarily for royal orders, they were organized on a small scale, but demanded both the highest professional ability and the most up-to-date technical equipment available from western Europe. No expense or effort was spared, and no commercial competition faced. The first Russian glass factory was started in 1688 by the Tsar Alexei Mikhailovich, with the

XXIX. Two papier mâché boxes, depicting a winter scene with peasants driving troikas. Lukutin, late 19th century.

help of Swedish experts. Peter the Great, at the beginning of the eighteenth century, founded another glass factory in Moscow, and later transferred it to Petersburg. He handed it over to his favourite, Menshikov, whose property was later confiscated, and thus reverted to the State. Catherine the Great presented the Imperial glass monopoly to her favourite Potemkin, but after his death she discreetly bought it back from his heirs. Inevitably it dominated the development of that branch of Russian decorative art throughout the eighteenth and early nineteenth centuries.

It is noteworthy that the greatest architects of Petersburg also did important work for the Imperial Glass Factory. Thomas de Thomon was chief designer there till he died in 1813. He was succeeded by the brilliant Rossi, who favourably influenced the design of massive chandeliers, for which Petersburg became famous. Rossi believed that a good architect must accept responsibility for every single detail of his building, and should design the interior lighting, furniture, and even door-handles. After Rossi came another leading architect, Voronikhin, who first started commercial sales of Imperial glass through special shops in Moscow, Petersburg, and Nijni-Novgorod.

Elaborate cut-glass goblets, engraved with floral sprays and crowned double-headed eagles, had been made for the Court ever since the reign of the Empress Elisabeth, and they were continued throughout the nineteenth century. These goblets often bear the monogram of the reigning monarch, engraved in the centre of the Imperial emblem (Plate 152A). In the last decades of the eighteenth century an opaque milky glass, made with an admixture of minutely ground bones, came into fashion. It provided an attractive novel background for painting, and has a distinctive style and rarity (Plate 154). The best designers from the Imperial Porcelain Factory were often employed to work out suitable shapes for glass objects, and these were sometimes combined with fine silver craftsmanship (Plate 154).

During the reigns of Alexander I and Nicolas I many monumental chandeliers and majestic mirrors were ordered for the palaces. In 1819 Alexander commissioned and presented to the Shah of Persia an elaborate crystal bath. The Shah was so delighted with it that he asked the Emperor to give him next time a spacious crystal double-bed, to complete the *ensemble*. The same period saw the use of transfer printing, especially of portrait heads, as a technical innovation, applied to decorated cut glass. This practice became widespread in the reign of Nicolas I, and produced some pleasing new results (Plate 153, see N. Kachalov, *Steklo*, p. 259, Moscow, 1959). The clear-cut monumental shapes, used even for small glass objects, still gave them grandeur and distinction.

After 1850 the technique of glass-making continued to progress in scientific capability, though it declined in taste. The setback of the Crimean War started a period of Imperial parsimony, and after the accession of Alexander II orders for fine artistic glass, to adorn the palaces, steadily decreased. Luckily for the decorative arts, this phase of royal puritanism was resisted by the new-rich middle class, which about this time started to formulate their own demand for more opulent and variegated colours, a fashion which later found reflection in products of the Imperial Factory. This intensely glowing and colourful glass came out most effectively in a new technique, introduced from Germany, which superimposed three layers of glass in different shades, inside transparent, outside strongly coloured, and in the middle a milky opaque tone.

But unrestrained craving for sheer luxury and vulgar ostentation ended by flouting the laws of proportion, though certain stricter standards were maintained in the Imperial factories until the end. For every single piece of glass produced for the palaces still had to be unique, and to meet with personal royal approval. Once a year the Director brought all important new pieces to Tsarskoe Selo, to be inspected there by the Tsar and members of his family. Sometimes the Director brought a second version of one big vase or bowl, about the perfect execution of which he had felt doubts, and displayed them side by side. As soon as the Imperial judges decided which of the two was better, the Director would break the inferior one into fragments with a hammer.

In 1890 the Imperial Glass Factory ceased to exist independently, and became merged with the Porcelain Factory. Not only good German technique but bad German aesthetic peculiarities began to prevail there. No doubt the German-born but uncultured Empress Alexandra Fyodorovna dictated in matters of taste to her husband, Nicolas II, and she must be held partly responsible for the deplorably low artistic level of both the porcelain and glass factories at the beginning of the twentieth century. *Art nouveau* incrustations of heavy water lilies and foliage were used to cover tortuously shaped objects, tinted in anaemic colours. Only the exact replacement of broken pieces made in previous reigns helped to maintain the higher quality of the past. And the Imperial family still ordered hundreds of traditionally shaped and painted glass and porcelain Easter eggs for presentation every Easter.

XXX. (*above*) Church of St Basil on the Red Square, Moscow. (*below*) View of the Kremlin
from the Moscow River. Lukutin, mid-19th century.

The Imperial Glass Factory continued to produce for a few years after the October Revolution, but finally closed down in 1920, when the fires of its furnaces were extinguished.

Another distinctive Russian art, though dating only from the eighteenth century, consisted in the carving or inlaying of native semi-precious stones for objects of interior decoration. This work displayed to advantage the inherent beauty of colour and patterned grain in malachite, lapis lazuli, jasper, Siberian jade, quartz, rhodonite, violet and red porphyry (Plate 155A and B). It became a luxurious genre, unrivalled anywhere in Europe, but it was, to start with, dependent on imported Italian craftsmen. It received a dazzling opportunity to develop during the building of the new capital, St Petersburg, in the eighteenth century, and it continued to flourish throughout the nineteenth century.

The leading architects of Italian origin, like Quarenghi, Rinaldi, and Rossi, accustomed in their native land to use a multitude of richly coloured stones or marble for constructing grand staircases and mosaic floors for entrance halls, found new scope for local Russian stone to adorn the great Petersburg palaces and public buildings. In the Ural Mountains and the Altai region vast deposits of semi-precious coloured stones had been discovered in the eighteenth century. They were extensively used for making vases, urns, table-tops, bowls, and *torchères*. Peter the Great's stone-polishing factory at Peterhof is known to have been directed for thirty years (1748–78) by a certain Joseph Bottom, the son of an adventurous English sailor, who had settled down in Russia.

The eminent architect, Alexander Bryulov, brother of the famous painter, indulged his own passion for malachite on a grand scale, when he restored the reception rooms of the Winter Palace, which had been destroyed by fire in 1837. He used solid and inlaid malachite not only for the walls and columns of the resplendent Malachite Hall, but for turning into vases, *torchère* lamps, and tables. A factory devoted almost exclusively to preparing articles inlaid with malachite, founded at Ekaterinburg in 1765, specialized in huge orders of this kind, and made whole walls covered with a finely patterned mosaic of malachite particles. It also produced colossal malachite, lapis lazuli, and jasper vases, with gilded bronze handles, to stand at focal points on grand staircases or in the alcoves of spacious reception rooms. The Emperor Nicolas I presented Queen Victoria with one of these splendid, nearly six-foot-high, malachite vases, when he came to stay at Windsor Castle in 1844 (Plate 155A).

261

The heavily prosaic and humdrum utilitarian tone, which crept through Russian society after 1861, led to a rapid deterioration both in the artistic quality and quantity of monumental objects made from Russian semi-precious stones. Orders from the Emperor and the impoverished aristocracy declined, and the new-rich industrial class, although they enjoyed display, lacked (with a few notable exceptions) a taste for grandeur allied with simple dignity. They showed a finer taste for small objects, though they often paid undue attention to fussy ornamental detail and gaudy opulence. But a constant and more fastidious demand for smaller decorative *objets d'art* remained alive throughout the nineteenth century, growing most vigorous towards the end of it.

The best of these objects were the brilliantly enamelled or nielloed silver and jewellery of Fabergé, Ovchinikov, Khlebnikov, and Sazykov. (See Chapter Two.) Outstanding also, were the exquisitely painted and lacquered papier mâché boxes illustrated in this chapter. Less familiar, but also unique of their kind, were carved malachite candelabra and dishes (Plate 156), and miniature figures in gilded bronze of Russian peasant types (Plates 147, 148), and historical figures, set on malachite or lapis lazuli stands. Many of these bronzes are superbly modelled, combining sensitive texture and feeling with movement and static poise. They reveal that rarely expressed ability, to make sculpture in the round, inherent in some gifted Russian artists, who found no scope or satisfaction in making official monuments.

facing, above

xxxi. Painted boxes (*top left to right*) Tea-drinking. Young soldier meeting a girl. Peasant woman with a wheelbarrow and two children. (*below*) Betrothal scene. Lukutin and Vishnyakov, mid-19th century.

facing, below

xxxii. Two large papier mâché boxes, depicting village maidens throwing garlands in the stream. Lukutin, early 19th century.

139A. (*above*) Boxwood carving, representing the Last Supper. Mid-19th century.
139B. (*below*) Carved wooden mould for stamping gingerbread with Imperial double-headed eagle.
Late 18th century. *Private collection, London.*

140. Carved wooden picture frame of family portrait, made by a serf artist for a Russian country house. First half of 19th century.

141. Chairs and table, painted with traditional designs in red and gold. Mid-19th century.

142B. Steel chair made in Tula. 18th century. *Victoria and Albert Museum, London.*

142A. Tula steel fireplace, probably made for England. Late 18th century. *Victoria and Albert Museum, London.*

143. Table in gilded carved wood, made by Russian craftsmen working in the style of Louis XVI. It bears the monogram of the Empress Maria Fyodorovna, consort of Paul I. Late 18th century.
Gatchina Palace.

---

facing page

144. Double-fronted chest in ebony, encrusted with floral scrolls in gilded bronze. Bosses in centre of each panel are carved from solid blocks of *lapis lazuli*. Dated 1873.
Collection, Mrs May, Washington, D.C.

145. Pottery *kvass*-jug, decorated with human heads. 18th century. *State Historical Museum, Moscow.*

146. Pottery *kvass*-jug, decorated with modelled birds and covered with green glaze. Mid-19th century. *State Historical Museum, Moscow.*

147. Pair of gilded bronze figures, a dancing peasant boy and girl, set on a malachite base. Second half of 19th century.

facing page

148A (*above*). Two dancing peasant boys in gilded bronze on malachite stands. Second half of 19th century.

148B (*below*). Two traditional carved and painted wooden arches, placed over horses' necks. (*below*) Bronze *troika*, with three prancing horses drawing a sleigh. E. A. Lanseré, late 19th century.

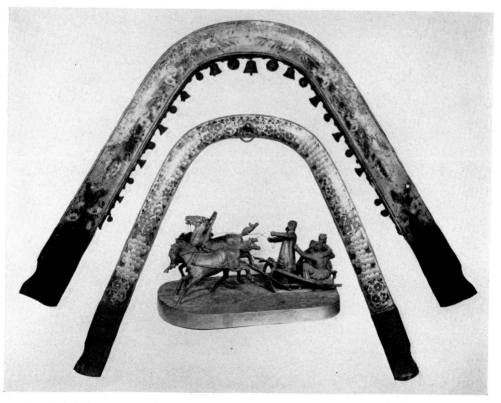

149. The Emperor Alexander II in the uniform of a general of the Cossack Bodyguard Regiment.
Bronze by an unknown artist. A replica is in the museum of the Imperial Cossack Bodyguard Regiment
at Courbevoie, Paris.

150. Portrait bust in ivory of the Empress Maria Fyodorovna, consort of Alexander III. Dated 1882.
Collection, Mrs May, Washington, D.C.

151. Carved ivory goblet from Archangel, featuring busts of
Russian Empresses. 18th century. *The Hermitage, Leningrad.*

152A. (*above*) Two 18th century cut-glass goblets, engraved with Imperial double-headed eagles, on the left with the monogram of the Empress Elisabeth.

152B. (*below*) Two cut-glass oblong decanters, engraved with Imperial emblems and monogram of Catherine II.

153. Specimens of glass from Imperial Glass Factory, Petersburg. (*left*) Gold-painted vodka glass with massive base. Late 18th century. (*centre*) Finely proportioned champagne glass with ruby-red bowl. Early 19th century. (*right*) Gold-painted beaker, decorated with a portrait of the consort of Nicolas I, printed in transfer. Mid-19th century.

154. (*left*) Wine jug engraved with a snipe, standing amid foliage, with another snipe, cast in silver, on the cover. Mid-19th century. (*right*) Liqueur decanter in milky white glass, painted with flies, made to celebrate the defeat of Napoleon in 1812.

155A. (*above*) Massive malachite vase, presented by Nicolas I to Queen Victoria, when he stayed at Windsor Castle in 1844. Height 5 ft. 10 in. *State Apartments, Windsor. Reproduced by kind permission of H.M. The Queen.*

155B. (*below*) Tray in dark green nephrite (Siberian jade) with chased silver-gilt handles, inlaid with strawberry-coloured enamel and set with diamonds. One of Fabergé's large works (17½ in. long). *Wernher Collection, Luton Hoo.*

156. Pair of late 19th century malachite candelabra and *tazzas*, seen against mid-19th century tapestry carpet (an Imperial order) depicting the coats of arms of numerous Russian towns.
Collection, Mrs May, Washington, D.C.

Select Bibliography

CHAPTER ONE: ICONS

Anisimov, A., *Les Anciennes Icones*, Fondation Piot, Paris, 1929.

Avinov, A. (Ed.), *Russian Icons in the Collection of George H. Hann*, Carnegie Institute, Pittsburgh, 1944.

Farbman, M. (Ed.), *Masterpieces of Russian Painting*, London, 1930.

Gerhard, H. P., *Welt der Ikonen*, Recklinghausen, 1963.

Kjellin, H., Aschberg Collection of Icons in the National Museum, Stockholm, 1956. (In Swedish.)

Kondakov, N., *The Russian Icon*, 4 vols., Prague, 1928–33. (In Russian.)

Kondakov, N., *The Russian Icon*, Oxford, 1937. (English summary of the preceding work.)

Kondakov, N., *Iconography of the Virgin Mary*, St Petersburg, 1914–15. (In Russian.)

Lazarev, V., *The Art of Novgorod*, Moscow, 1947. (In Russian.)

Lazarev, V., *Theopanes the Greek and his School*, Moscow, 1961. (In Russian.)

Likhachev, N. P., *Materials for a History of Russian Icon Painting*, 2 vols., 419 plates, Leipzig and St Petersburg, 1906. (In Russian.)

Muratov, P., *Old Russian Icons in the Collection of I. S. Ostroukhov*, Moscow, 1914. (In Russian.)

Muratov, P., *L'Ancienne Peinture Russe*, Rome and Prague, 1925.

Rice, D. Talbot, *Russian Icons*, London and New York, 1947.

U.N.E.S.C.O. World Art Series, *Early Russian Icons*, New York, 1958.

Uspensky, A. I., *The Tsar's Icon Painters and Painters of the Seventeenth Century*, Moscow, 1914. (In Russian.)

Uspensky, L., and Lossky, V., *Der Sinn der Iconen*, Berne, 1952.

Weidle, W., *Les Icones Byzantines et Russes*, Florence, 1950.

Wulff, O., and Alpatov, M., *Denkmäler der Iconenmalerei*, Hellerau bei Dresden, 1925.

Zolotnitsky, J., *Trente-Cinq Primitifs Russes*, Paris, 1931.

SELECT BIBLIOGRAPHY

CHAPTER TWO: SILVER

Bäcksbacka, L., *St Petersburgs Juvelerare, 1714–1870*, Helsingfors, 1951.

Bainbridge, H. C., *Peter Carl Fabergé, his Life and Work*, London, 1949.

Benois, A., and Prakhov, A., *Art Treasures of Russia*, 5 vols., St Petersburg, 1901–5. (In Russian and French.)

Bunt, C., *Russian Art*, London, 1949.

Foelkersam, A., *Inventaire des Palais Impériaux*, St Petersburg, 1907.

Maskell, A., *Russian Art*, London, 1886.

Porfiridov, N., *Russian Silver and Enamel, Russian Museum, Leningrad*, Leningrad, 1956. (In Russian.)

Postnikova-Loseva, and Platonova, M., *Russian Artistic Silver, State Historical Museum, Moscow*, Moscow, 1959. (In Russian.)

Rosenberg, M., *Der Goldschmiede Merkzeichen*, Frankfurt, 1911.

Snowman, K., *The Art of Carl Fabergé*, London, 1958.

Trutevsky, W., and Kersch, E., basic articles on Russian seventeenth-century silver in *Starye Gody*, monthly art journal in Russian, St Petersburg, 1910.

Antiquities of the Russian Empire, 6 folio volumes, St Petersburg, 1852. (In Russian.)

Argenterie Russe Ancienne de la Collection Eugène Lubovich, Paris, 1932 (privately printed).

Guide to Artistic Silver in the Hermitage, Moscow, 1956. (In Russian.)

CHAPTER THREE: EARLY PORTRAIT PAINTING

Diaghilev, S., *Russian Painting in the 18th century*, St Petersburg, 1901. (In Russian.)

Gollerbach, *Portrait Painting in Russia*, Moscow, 1923. (In Russian.)

Gorlenko, V., *D. Levitsky*, St Petersburg, 1901. (In Russian.)

Kuzminsky, K., *S. Rokotov and D. Levitsky*, Moscow, 1939. (In Russian.)

Lebedev, G., *Russian Painting in the early 18th century*, Moscow, 1938. (In Russian.)

Mashkovets, N., *V. Borovikovsky*, Moscow, 1950. (In Russian.)

Nicolas Mikhailovich, Grand-Duke (Ed.), *Russian Portraits of the 18th and 19th centuries*, St Petersburg, 1905–9. (In Russian.)
Stariye Gody (monthly periodical in Russian).
L. Caravaque in Russia (June 1908). *Foreign Painters in Russia* (June–September 1912).

CHAPTER FOUR: PORCELAIN

Emme, B., *Russian Art Porcelain*, Moscow-Leningrad, 1950. (In Russian.)
Lukomsky, G., *Russisches Porzellan*, Berlin, 1924.
Roche, D., and Issaievitch, I., *Exposition de Céramiques Russes Anciennes*, Catalogue, Musée de Sèvres, Paris, 1929.
Rozembergh, A., *Les Marques de la Porcelaine Russe*, Paris, 1926.
Selivanov, A., *Porcelain and Pottery of the Russian Empire*, with illustrations of all known factory marks, Vladimir, 1903. (In Russian.)
The Imperial Porcelain Factory, 1744–1904, published by the Administration, St Petersburg, 1904–6. (In Russian with a French summary, richly illustrated.)
Catalogue of Russian Porcelain in the collection of N. A. Lukutin, Moscow, 1901. (In Russian.)
The State Porcelain Factory, edited by I. Rodin, Leningrad, 1938. (In Russian.)

CHAPTER FIVE: EARLY NINETEENTH CENTURY PAINTERS

Alekseyeva, T., *Artists of the School of Venetsianov*, Moscow-Leningrad, 1958. (In Russian.)
Alpatov, M., *Alexander Ivanov*, Moscow, 1956. (In Russian.)
Atsarkina, E., *O. Kiprensky*, Moscow, 1948. (In Russian.)
Diaghilev, S., *Catalogue of the Historical-Artistic Exhibition of Russian Portraits in the Tauride Palace* (8 vols.), St Petersburg, 1905. (In Russian.)

Leonov, A. (Ed.), *Sketches of the life and work of Russian artists in the first half of the 19th century*, Moscow, 1954. (In Russian.)

Lyaskovskaya, O., *K. Bryulov*, Moscow, 1940. (In Russian.)

Nicolas Mikhailovich, Grand-Duke (Ed.), *Russian Portraits of the 18th and 19th centuries* (5 vols.), St Petersburg, 1905–9. (In Russian.)

Vrangel, N. O., *A. Kiprensky*, St Petersburg, 1912. (In Russian.)

Vrangel, N. O., *A. Venetsianov in Private Collections*, St Petersburg, 1911. (In Russian.)

CHAPTER SIX: LATE NINETEENTH AND EARLY TWENTIETH
CENTURY PAINTERS

Benois, A., *The Russian School of Painting*, St Petersburg, 1904. (In Russian.)

Fiala, V., *Russian Paintings*, Prague, 1955.

Friehe, V. M., *Russian Painting in the 19th Century*, Moscow, 1929. (In Russian.)

Glagol, S., and Grabar, I., *I. Levitan*, Moscow, 1912. (In Russian.)

Gor, S., and Petrov, V., *V. Surikov*, Moscow, 1935. (In Russian.)

Grabar, I., *Serov, his Life and Work*, Moscow, 1913. (In Russian.)

Grabar, I., *Repin*, 2 vols., Moscow-Leningrad, 1948–9. (In Russian.)

Hamilton, G. H., *The Art and Architecture of Russia*, London, 1954.

Korostin, A., *Russian Lithographs of the 19th Century*, Moscow, 1953. (In Russian.)

Lebedev, A., and Burov, G., *Correspondence of V. Vereshchagin and V. Stasov*, Moscow, 1951. (In Russian.)

Leshchinsky, Y., *P. A. Fedotov*, Moscow-Leningrad, 1946. (In Russian.)

Shchekotov, N., *The Pictures of V. Surikov*, Moscow, 1944. (In Russian.)

Shcherbatov, Prince, *An Artist in Vanished Russia*, New York, 1955. (In Russian.)

Sobko, N. P., *V. G. Perov, his Life and Work*, St Petersburg, 1892. (In Russian.)

Talbot Rice, T. *A Concise History of Russian Art*, London, 1964.

Yaremich, S., *M. A. Vrubel*, Moscow, 1911. (In Russian.)

CHAPTER SEVEN: DECORATIVE ARTS

Bakushinsky, A., *The Art of Palekh*, Moscow-Leningrad, 1934. (In Russian.)

Bobrinski, A., *Popular Russian Wooden Crafts*, Moscow, 1911. (In Russian.)

Efimova, E., *Russian Carved Stone in the Hermitage*, Leningrad, 1961. (In Russian.)

Holme, C. (Ed.), *Peasant Art in Russia, The Studio*, London, Paris, 1912.

Kachalov, N., *Glass*, Moscow, 1959. (In Russian.)

Kryukova, I., *Russian Popular Carving in Bone*, Moscow, 1959. (In Russian.)

Large Soviet Encyclopaedia, Vol. 44, p. 579, *The Fedoskino Miniature*. (In Russian.)

Nekrasov, A., *Russian Peasant Art*, Moscow, 1924. (In Russian.)

Popova, C., *Russian Popular Ceramics*, Moscow, 1957. (In Russian.)

Saltykov, A. (Ed.), *Russian Popular Ceramics*, Moscow, 1960. (In Russian.)

Yalovenko, G., *Fedoskino*, Moscow, 1959. (In Russian.)

Index

Abramtsevo, 253
Ador, 74
Alexander I, 144, 145, 171, 174, 175, 226, 259, Pl. 44
Alexander II, 147, 149, 218, 258, 260, Pl. 149
Alexander III, 154
Alexandra Fyodorovna, Empress, 260
Alexei Mikhailovich, Tsar, 34, 35, 36, 73, 258
Allahabad, 226
Alpatov, M., 185
Altai, 261
Andreyev, N., 35fn.
Antiquities of the Russian Empire, 72, 75, 217
Antropov, A., 115, 120, Pls. 68, 69
Apollo, Hyacinth and Kiparis, 183
Appearance of the Messiah before the people, 184, 185, Pls. 115 A and B
Apraksin, Countess, 115, Pl. 68
Aquatints, 212
Arabesque Service, 144
Archangel Gabriel, 37, Pl. 17
Archangel Michael, 29–30, 37
Arkhangelskoe, 145
Armoury, *see* State Armoury
Artist who, relying on his talent, married without a dowry, 210
Ascension, The, 30, Pl. 9
Asia Minor, 23, 181
Athens, 175, 228
Augsburg, 74
Avakum, 35, 36
Ayvazovsky, I., 212, Pl. 118 A

Bakst, L., 228–9, Pl. 136
Ballets russes, 224

Bargemen, The, 219
Barn, The, 176, 177, 178
Batenin (factory), 152
Bell, The, 185
Benkendorf, Count, A. 174
Benois, A. N., 224, 227
Berlin, 214
Bezborodko, Count, 117, 144
Blessing of the Regimental Banners in front of the restored Winter Palace, 207
Bogdanov-Byelsky, N., 213, Pl. 129
Bologna, 175
Boris Godunov, 224
Borovikovsky, V., 39, 117, 118, 119, 120, 175, 176, 227, Pls. 73–75
Böttger, 140
Bottom, Joseph, 261
Boucher, F., 117
Boyarinya Morozova, 218, Pl. 121
Bratina, 71, 72, Pls. 35 A and B
Bronze modelling, 258, 262
Brunswick, 257
Bryulov, A., 179, 261, Pl. xxiv
Bryulov, K., 172, 173, 174, 178–2, 186, 207, 208, 211, Pls. 109–13
Bryusov, V., 223
Buslaev, T., 27
Byron, R., 25fn
Byzantine art, 23, 27, 28, 29, 30, 31, 32, 37, 38, 68, 69, 75, 76, 78, 221, 226
Byzantine neo-Hellenism, 28, 29, 30
Byzantium, 25, 31, 68

Cabinet Service, 144
Caravaque, L., 115
Card-Players, 207

Carnaval, 229

Carving: ivory, 28, 258; peasant, 251, 252

Cathedrals: Archangel (Kremlin), 32, 73; Annunciation (Kremlin), 29, 32; Dmitrievsky (Vladimir), 27; Dormition (Kremlin), 35, (Vladimir), 29; Kazan (Petersburg), 119; St. Andrew's (Kiev), 115, 120; St. Basil (Moscow), 218, 256; St. Isaac's (Petersburg), 182; St. Sophia (Constantinople), 23, (Kiev), 28, (Novgorod), 27; Uspensky (Kremlin), 32

Catherine I, 115, 116, Pl. 65

Catherine II (the Great), 38, 74, 117, 118, 119, 120, 141, 144, 147, 149, 226, 259, Pl. 72 B

Caucasus, 219

Central Asia, 150, 219, 226

Chagall, M., 228

Chaliapin, F., 220, Pl. 131 A

Châtelet Theatre, 224

Chekhov, A., 213

Cherkassov, Baron, 140, 141

Chernyshevsky, N., 185, 213, 217

China and Chinese art, 27, 71, 72, 140, 142

Chirin, P., 32

Christ, 24, 28, 31, 32, 36, 37, 184, 217, 251

Christ appearing to Mary Magdalene, 183

Christ in the Garden of Gethsemane, 216

Church (Orthodox), 23, 24, 25, 30, 33, 34, 35, 36, 70, 73, 217, 254

Cimabue, 29

Cleopatra, 229

Clérisseau, C., 141

Cloisonné, 70

Cochran, J. B., 225

Commedia dell 'Arte, 149

Constantinople, 23, 26, 27, 28, 29, 31, 181

Contemporary, The, 185

Copenhagen, 142, 147

Coq d'Or, Le, 228

Crimean War, 215, 260

Crucifixion, The, 34, Pl. II, Pl. 20

Dashkov, Princess, 120, Pl. 76

Danilkovo, 255, 257

Davidov, Y., 173, Pl. 100

da Vinci, Leonardo, 173, 221

Dawe, G., 181

Death of the wounded Lensky, 216

Decadents in the Academy, 228

Decembrists, 177

Decorative arts, 254–62

Demidov, A., 178

Demon, The, 222, 223, Pl. 134

de St. Pierre, B., 152

Desnitsky, Metropolitan M., 119, Pl. 75

de Thomon, T., 259

de Velly, J., 116

Diaghilev, S., 34, 119, 121, 224–5, 226, 227

Diderot, 121

Discriminating Bride, The, 208

Dmitry, Tsarevich, 73, Pl. 34

Dionysius, 30, Pl. 8

Dobujinsky, M., 227

Don Cossacks, 31

Dostoyevsky, F., 21, 215

Dresden, 214

Duccio, A., 29

Dutch art, 147, 179, 208, 210

Dyakonov, A., 172

Easter Procession, 215

Eastern art, 24, 30, 31, 68

Egypt, 23

Ekaterinburg, 261

Elisabeth, Empress, 74, 115, 116, 117, 140, 148, 174, 259

Emancipation of 1861, 145, 147, 222, 253, 262

Enamel, 32, 38, 39, 69, 70, 75

England, 147

Engraving, 212, 217, 253

Fabergé, Carl, 72, 75, 76, 77, 78, 262, Pl. XII, Pls. 38, 61 B, 62

Fedoskino, 255–7

Fedoskino Craftsmens' Guild of former artists of the Lukutin Factory, 257
Fedotov, P., 207–11, 214, 258, Pl. 117
Filigree, 69, 70, 75
Finland, 74
Florence, 175, 180
Fragonard, 117
France, 114, 116, 117, 141, 171
Frescoes, 23, 27, 30, 223, 225
Furniture, 254
Fürstenberg (factory), 154

Gagarin, Prince G., 181, Pl. 114
    Princesses Helen and Alexandra, 119, Pl. 74
Gainsborough, 119
Gardner, Alexei, 150
Gardner (factory), 149, 150, 151, 152, 153, 176, 258
Gatchina, 144
Gattenberg, 149
Gé, N., 217
Geneva, 121
Georgi, J., 142
Gérard, F., 173
Germany, 74, 179, 260
Girl picking grapes, 179, Pl. 112
Girl placing a candle in the church, 178, Pl. 108
Gjelsk region, 149, 254
Glass, 258–61
Gogol, N., 180, 183, 208
Gold work, 70, 71, 73, 74; hallmarks, 77; standard, 77
Golden Fleece, The, 224
Golovin, A., 224, 227
Goncharova, N., 228
Gorbunov, 151
Gorchakov, Prince, 118
Gorky, M., 154
Gouache, 227
Goya, 186
Grabar, I., 217

Granet, 177
Great Fire (1547), 33
Great Schism, 25, 30, 36
Greece, 27, 29, 31, 37, 69, 73, 181, 228
Grimm, 141
Gubkin (silversmith), 110
Guilds (craftsmens), 74

Hanseatic towns, 28, 70
Harlamov, A., 211, Pl. 124 B
Harvesting, The, 176, 177, Pl. 103
Head of an Angel, 27, Pl. 2
Herculaneum, 144
Hermitage, 118, 141, 146, 147, 173, 176, 177, 178, 179, 185, 210, 215
Herzen, A., 185
Himalayan Research Institute, 226
Historical Museum, Moscow, 218
Hitrovo, B., 34, 35, 36, 73, 201
Hogarth, 208, 210
Holland, 114
Holy Synod, 39
Homer, 182
Houghton Hall, 118
Hunger, C. K., 140, 141
Hunter's Service, 142

Icons and icon-painting, 23–40, 114, 217, 255, 256
Icon of the Vernicle, 36, Pl. 21
Imperial Academy of Arts, 75, 116, 119, 120, 172, 175, 177, 178, 179, 181, 182, 183, 208, 210, 211, 214, 216, 221, 228
Imperial Ballet, 224
Imperial Glass Factory, 258–60
Imperial Porcelain Factory, 140–9, 152, 154, 176, 179, 258, 259, 260
Imperial Textile Factory, 258
Impressionists, French, 185, 220
India, 68, 78, 219, 226
Ingres, 186
International Exhibition 1851, 147
Islam and Islamic art, 30, 68, 73

Italian art and Italy, 114, 118, 141, 144, 149, 173, 179, 180, 182, 183, 185, 211, 261. Cf. Renaissance
Italian girl washing at a fountain, 179
Italian noon, 179, Pl. 112
Ivan III, 70
Ivan IV (the Terrible), 33, 72, 181
Ivan IV with the body of his son, 219
Ivan Ivanovich, Tsarevich, 72
Ivanov, Alexander, 182–6, 211, Pls. 115 A and B
Ivanov, Andrey, 182
Ivanov, Paul, 146

John the Baptist, 184
Journal of Caricatures, 176

Kachalov, N., 260
Kaendler, J., 142
Karamzin, N., 181
Kazan, 181, 257
Kestner, 149
Khlebnikov (silversmith), 75, 262
Kholuy, 39, 257
Kiev, 24, 27, 28, 69, 120, 221, 257
Kiprensky, O., 172, 173, 174, 181, 186, Pls. 99–102
Kondakov, N., 23, 28, 38, 69, 217
Kornilov (factory), 153
Korobov, P., 255, 257
Korovin, K., 227
Kostroma, 69
Kovsch, 71, 76, Pls. 36, 37, 38
Kozlov (factory), 12
Kramskoy, I. N., 215, 216, 217
Kremlin, 32, 71, 73, 256
Krylov, 207, 221
Kudinov (factory), 145
Kushelev, Count G. G., 172, 174
Kushelev, Countess, 119
Kustodiev, B., 227, Pl. xxv
Kuznetsov (porcelain combine), 149, 151, 153

Lacquer work, 40, 254, 256, 257; on silver, 75
Lagrenée, L., 116, 120
Lampi, J. B. (the elder), 117, 118, 119, Pl. 72 A
Lanseré, E. A., 258
Last Day of Pompeii, The, 180, 182, Pl. 111
Last Judgement, 27
Lawrence, Thomas, 181
Le Brun, Mme. Vigée, 117
Le Lorrain, 116
Lenin, 154
Lermontov, M., 222
Levitan, I., 213
Levitsky, D., 115, 117–20, 227, Pls. 76–80
Levshina, Alexandra, 120, Pl. 77
Likhachev, N. P., 26, 217
Little Widow, The, 210
London, 147, 185, 219
Louis XV, 116, 117
Louis XVI, 117, 254
Lukutin, N., 257
Lukutin, P., 255, 256, 257
Lyubavin (silversmith), 75, Pl. xiv

Maeterlinck, M., 226
Magic Lantern, 176
Majolica, 254
Major's Courtship, The, 208, Pl. 117
Makovsky, V. Y., 213
Malachite, 261, 262
Mamontov, S., 222
Marburg, 141
Maria Fyodorovna, Empress, 275
Marx, Karl, 154
Matveyev, A., 114, 115
Maykov, A. N., 215
Meissen (factory), 140, 142, 144, 146, 149, 150, 154
Menshikov, A. D., 259
Metal-work, 32, 68–78. Cf. Gold work; silver work; filigree
Michael, Tsar, 72

Michael Petrovich, Grand Duke, 207
Michelangelo, 180, 182, 221
Mikhailov, G., 178
Miklashevsky (factory), 145
Milan, 173
Miller, G., 149
Milli, Karl, 152
Mirgorod, 119
Mir Isskustva (World of Art), 224, 226, 227, 228
Mochalov, P. S., 172
Monasteries: Pecherskaya Lavra, 120; Spasso-Andryonikov, 29; Therapont, 30; Trinity Sergius, 29
Mongol conquest, 28, 69
Month in the Country, A., 227, Pl. 137
Moral and Critical Scenes from daily life, 210
Moreau, Jean, 116
Morkov, Count, 175
Morning of a Lady Landowner, 176
Morning of an Official, 208
Morozov (silversmith), 75
Morozov, M., 220
Morozov, S., 253
Morozov Fund, 257
Mosaics, 23, 221
Moscow, 25, 27, 29, 31, 32, 33, 34, 35, 69, 70, 71, 73, 75, 77, 78, 151, 176, 207, 215, 217, 218, 222, 224, 257, 259
Moscow Art Theatre, 227, 228
Moscow Cadet School, 207
Moscow Ceramic Exhibition, 153
Mount Athos, 29, 73
Mstera, 39, 40, 257
Munich, 220
Muratov, P., 38
Mussorgsky, M., 219, 224, Pl. 128

Naples, 173, 175
Napoleon, 73, 146, 171, 172, 219
Napoleonic Wars, 145, 152
Narcissus, 229
Narodniki, 213, 251

Nattier, 117
Nazarov, A., 26, 27
Nekrasov, 214, 215
Nelidova, Catherine, 120, Pl. 78
Nesterov, M., 217
Nestor's Chronicle, 23
New York, 219, 226
Nicolas I, 75, 144, 146, 181, 183, 185, 207, 210, 217, 259, 261, Pl. 44
Nicolas II, 148, 154, 220, 260
Niello, 69, 73, 75
Nijinsky, 226
Nijni-Novgorod, 259
Nikitin, I., 114, 115
Nikon, Patriarch, 35, 36, 73
Novgorod, 24, 27, 28, 29, 30, 31, 32, 34, 69, 70

October Revolution, 154, 228, 261
Officer's life in the country, 211
Old Believers, 25, 35, 38, 218
Old Masters, 26, 146, 174, 177, 179, 181, 214
Old Testament Trinity, 29, Pl. 11
Olenin, A. N., 179
On the Boulevard, 213, Pl. 122
Orthodox Church—see Church
Oruzheinaya Palata (Kremlin), 71, 73
Ostankino, 116
Ostrovsky, A. N., 215
Ostrogorsk, 216
Our Lady of the Burning Bush, 31, Pl. 13
Ovchinikov (silversmith), 75, 77, 110, 262

Painting, 171–86; episodic *genre*, 213; *genre*, 119, 172, 175, 176, 210, 211, 214, 227, 228; landscape, 176, 178, 211, 212; miniature, 38, 71, 75, 145, 255, 256; the nude, 185; 'opaque' method, 256; Persian miniature, 30, 32; portrait, 39, 114–21, 172–5, 176, 178, 181, 186, 207, 217, 219, 220; portrait in enamel, 70, 71; religious *see* Icons; seascape, 212; 'transparent' method, 256; water colour, 227

Palekh, 39, 40, 257

Paleologue, 29

Papier mâché, 253, 255–7

Paris, 116, 117, 180, 211, 214, 219, 220, 224, 227

Parland, A., 218

Pastel, 176

Patriarchs, 71, 73, 78

Patterson, 212

Paul, Tsarevich, 118; Emperor, 120, 145, Pl. 49

Paul of Aleppo, 35

Pauzié, J., 74

Pavlova, Anna, 220, Pl. 132

Peasant art, 76, 251–8

Peking, 140

Pen-and-ink drawing, 227

Peredvizhniki, 216, 217

Perov, V., 214–16, 258, Pls. 125–6

Persian art, 30, 31, 32, 68, 72, 73, 78

Peter (the Great), 30, 36, 38, 74, 114, 140, 220, 259, 261, Pl. 65

Peter III, 115, 148, Pl. 69

Petersburg (St Petersburg), 39, 74, 75, 77, 78, 115, 145, 147, 152, 153, 172, 174, 175, 176, 178, 180, 181, 182, 185, 207, 208, 211, 215, 217, 223, 224, 226, 259, 261

Petersburg Academy, *see* Imperial Academy of Arts

Peterhof, 261

Petrushka, 227

Plotinus, 24

Pogodin, M. P., 215

Poltoratsky, Mme., 120, Pl. 80

Pompeii, 180

Poor Lisa, 174, Pl. 102

Popov, A. (factory) 152, 153, 257

Popov, D., 152

Porcelain, 140–54; marks, 148, 151, 152, 153

Portrait of the Shishmarev Sisters, 181, Pl. 113

Portrait of Vera Mamontov, 220, Pl. 130

Portraiture, *see* Painting—portrait

Post-impressionism, 226

Potemkin, G., 118, 259, Pl. 72 A

Pottery, peasant, 254, Pls. 145, 146

Poussin, 183

Prince Igor, 226

Pskov, 28, 31; siege of, 181

Pugachev Rebellion, 216

Punjab, 226

Pushkin, 171, 172, 175, 179, 180, 181, 182, 207, 258

Quarenghi, 261

Rachette, Jean, 142, 143

Raphael, 173, 180, 185, 186

Raphael Service, 147, Pl. XVII

Rastrelli, B. B. and K. B., 115

Ravens have arrived, The, 213, Pl. 123

Recklinghausen, 38

Red Square, 256

Rembrandt, 173, 186

Renaissance, 24, 29, 33, 37, 70, 73, 221

Reni, Guido, 180

Renoir, 220

Repin, I., 219, 220

Reynolds, Sir J., 221

Ribeaupierre, Ivan, 120, Pl. 79

Rice, D. Talbot, 25fn.

Rimsky-Korsakov, N. A., 228

Rinaldi, A., 261

Roerich, N., 226

Rokotov, F., 115, 117, Pl. 70

Rome, 147, 148, 173, 174, 175, 179, 182, 183, 184, 185, 211

Rörstrand factory, 140

Roslin, A., 117, 118, Pl. 72 B

Rossi, K. I., 259, 261

Rostopchin, Count, 172

Rostov Miracle Workers, 38, 39, Pl. VI

Roussel, P., 256

Rovinsky, D. A., 32, 217

Royal Workshops, 33

Rubens, 173, 179

Rublev, A., 25, 29, 30, Pl. I
Russian Museum (Leningrad), 117
Russo-Japanese War, 257
Russo-Turkish War, 219

Sacre du Printemps, Le, 226
St. Catherine the Martyr, 39, Pl. VII
St. Florus and St. Lavrus, 30, Pl. 10
St. George, 39
St. John the Baptist, 37, 223, Pl. 14
St. John with the Wings, 37, Pl. 24
St. Nicolas the miracle worker, 39, Pl. VII
St. Peter and St. Paul, 27, Pl. 3
St. Vladimir Order of Knighthood, 120
SS. Boris and Gleb, 39
SS. Florus, Lavrus and George, 38, Pl. v
Safronov (factory), 12
Samoilova, 181
Savrasov, A., 213
Saxony, 140, 149
Sazykov (silversmith), 75, 257, 262
Schumann, 229
Schwalbe, A. K., 172
Schwebach, 145
Scott, Walter, 180
Semi-precious stones, 261, 262
Serbia, 29
Serf craftsmen, 116, 117, 254
Serov, V., 220–21, Pls. 130, 131
Sèvres, 145, 146, 150, 152, 154
Shchukin, S. S., 175
Shah (of Persia), 259
Shéherazade, 229
Sheremetyev, Count D., 174, 257
Sheremetyev Family, 116
Sherwood, N., 218
Shishkov, A., 174
Shuvalov, Count P. A., 116, 118
Siberia, 31, 71, 218
Silver work, 32, 38, 68–78, 262; hallmarks, 74, 77; lacquered, 75; repoussé, 28, 33, 39; standard, 77
Sister Beatrice, 226

Sistine Chapel, 182
Skan, 69
Slav art, 29, 71, 75, 76, 175, 218
Sleeping Shepherd, The, 176, 177, Pl. 104
Smolny Institute, 120
Society for the Encouragement of Art, 179, 182
Society for Travelling Art Exhibitions, *see* Peredvizhniki, 216, 217
Solyvchegodsk, 31, 71
Somov, K., 227
Soroka, G., 178, Pl. 107
Soudeikin, S., 228
Spectre de la Rose, Le, 229
Spiess, 147
Stage décor and design, 222, 227, 228, 229
Stariye Gody, 224
Stasov, J., 228
State Armoury,, *see* Oruzheinaya Palata, 32, 34, 75
State Factory (porcelain), 154
Stolitsa i Usad'ba, 224
Stravinsky, I., 226, 227
Stroganovs, 31, 32, 71
Stryelkovsky, A., 213, Pl. 124 A
Surikov, V., 218, Pl. 121
Svenigorod, 29
Sweden, 74, 140

Talashkina, 253
Tannauer, G., 115, Pl. 67
Tartars, 28, 32, 34, 70
Tauride Palace, 121, 224
Tea-drinking, 215
Telesheva, K., 174
Tenisheva, Princess, 253
Theophanes the Greek, 29, Pl. 67
They did not expect him, 220
Thorwaldsen, B., 173
Tibet, 226
Tiepolo, 118
Time of Troubles, 34, 70
Tintoretto, 183, 228

Titian, 183
Tittoni, A., 182
Tocqué, L., 116, 117, Pl. 71 A
Tolstoy, L., 21, 217, 219, 251
Torelli, S., 118
Transfer printing (on glass), 259; (on porcelain), 146
Tretyakov, P., 72, 215
Tretyakov Gallery, 28, 29, 120, 178, 184, 223
Tropinin, V., 172, 175, Pl. 98, 106
Tsarskoe Selo, 141, 260
Tula, 254
Turgenev, I., 184, 211, 227
Turkey and Turks, 31, 144, 150, 181

Ukrainian artists, 31, 71
Ural Mountains, 261
Ushakov, S., 36, 37, 38, Pls. 21, 22

Valeriani, J., 120
Vandyck, 173, 179, 215
Velasquez, 179, 215
Venetsianov, A. G., 119, 172, 175–7, 178, 212, 214, 258, Pls. 103, 104, 105 B
Venice, 181, 183, 221
Vereshchagin, V., 218, Pl. 127
Vermeer, 215
Veronese, P., 181, 183
Vesuvius, 174
Viardot, Mme., 211
Victoria, Queen, 261
Vienna, 154, 219
Village artists, 39
Village Funeral, The, 215, Pl. 125

Vinogradov, D., 141
Viollet-le-Duc, E. E., 68
Virgin Mary, 24, 27, 31, 38, Pl. 6
Virgin of the Sign, 28, Pl. 4
Virgin of Vladimir, 26, 27, Pl. 1
Vishnyakov, 257
Vladimir, 27, 29
Vladimir, Prince of Kiev, 23
Vladimir-Suzdal, 28
Volokhitin, 145
Vorobyov, M., 212
Voronikhin, A. N., 259
Vrubel, M., 221–3, Pl. 133–5

Walking in Moscow under the rain, 207
Walpole, Lord, 118
Weber, 229
Western art, 28, 29, 33, 34, 35, 36, 37, 38, 39, 68, 74, 75, 76, 77, 78, 114, 115, 117, 140, 142, 144, 146, 171, 186, 211, 223, 253
What is Truth, 217
Windsor Castle, 261
Winter Palace, 181, 261
World of Art, The, *see Mir Isskustva*

Yakovlev, A., 228
Yaroslavl, 28, 31
Yermak, 218
Young girl against the background of a Persian carpet, 221, Pl. 133
Yusupov, Prince, 145

Zagoskin, M., 257
Zhukovsky, V. A., 172